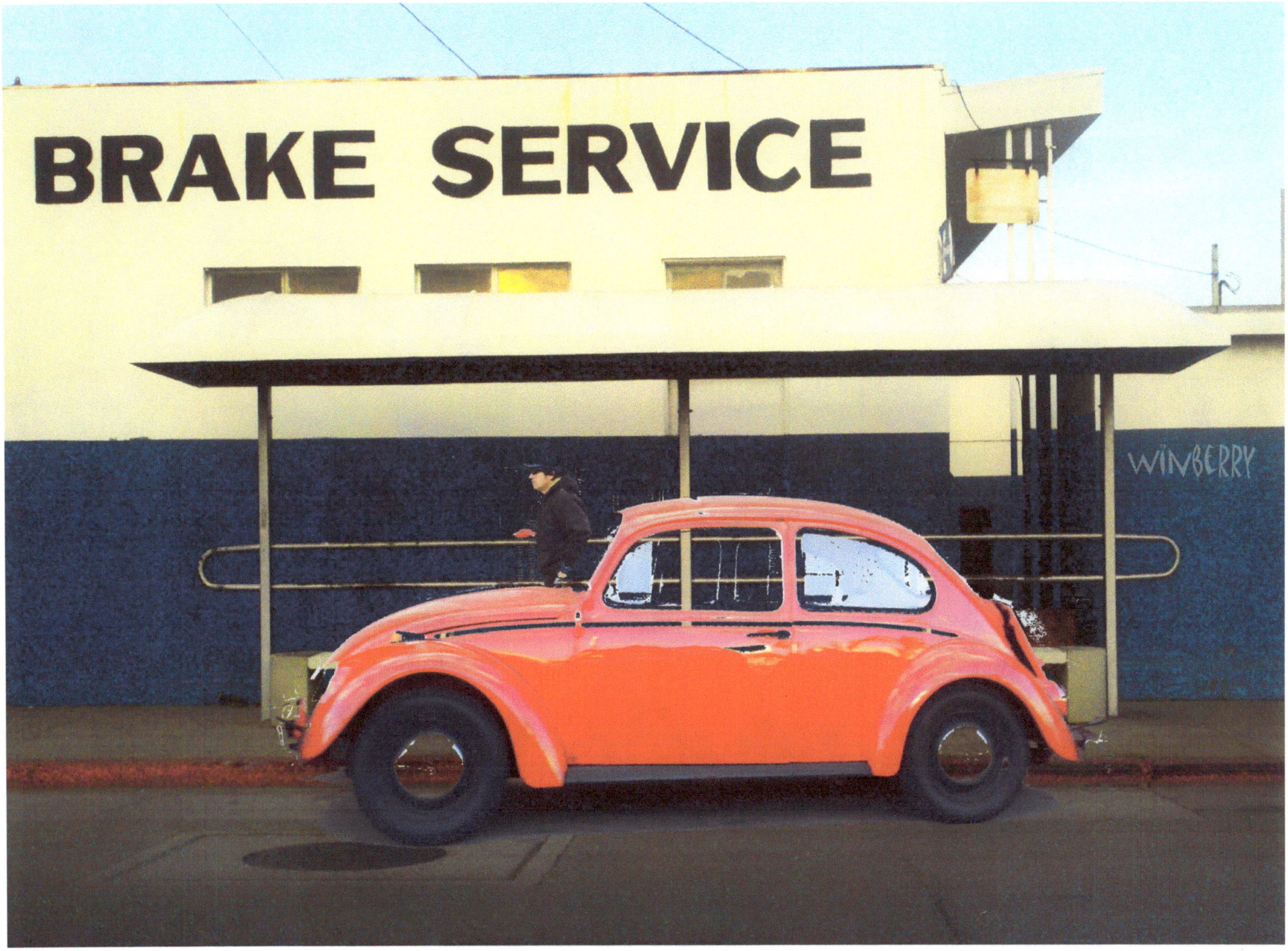
BRAKE SERVICE
WINBERRY

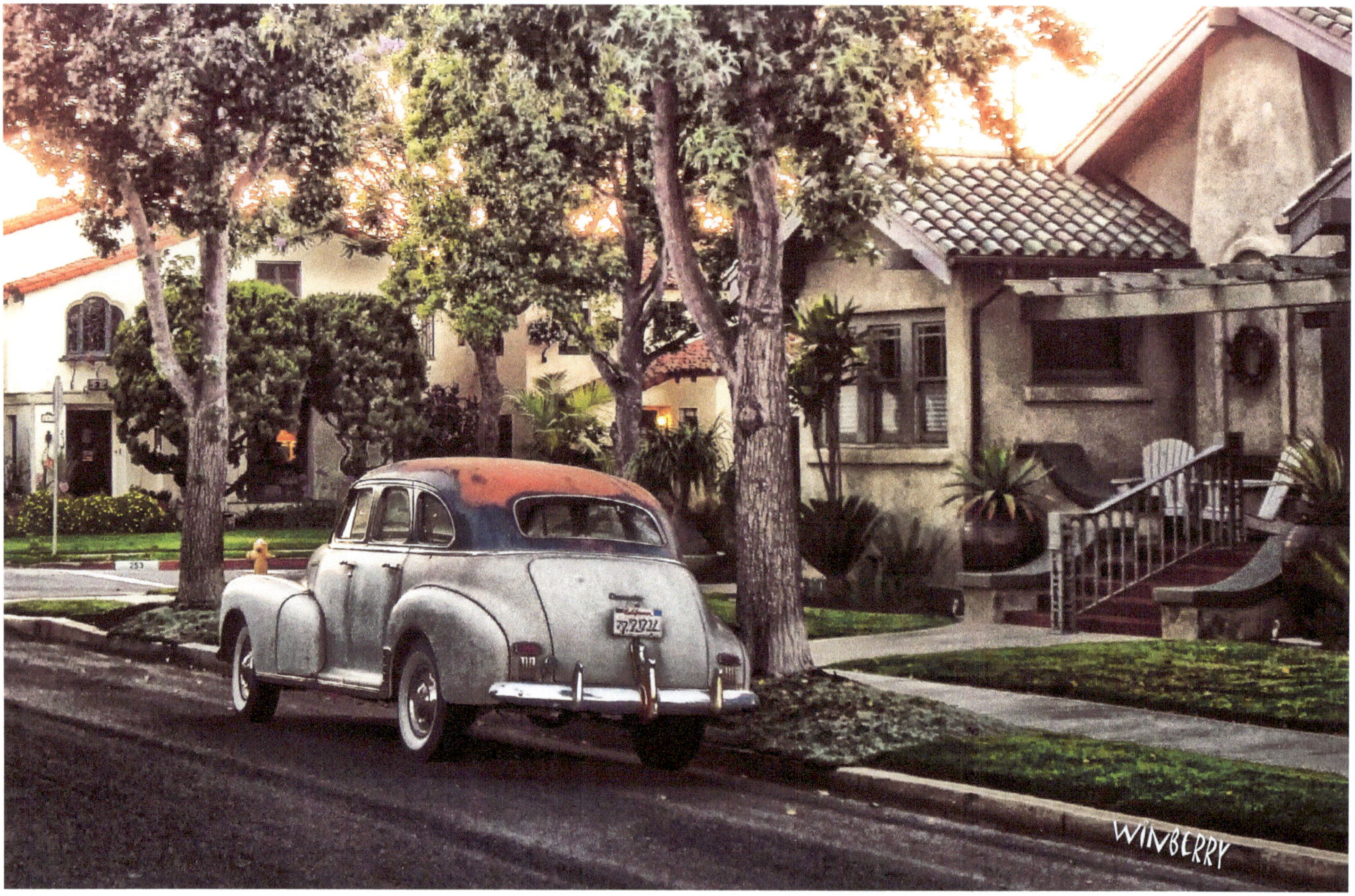
WINBERRY

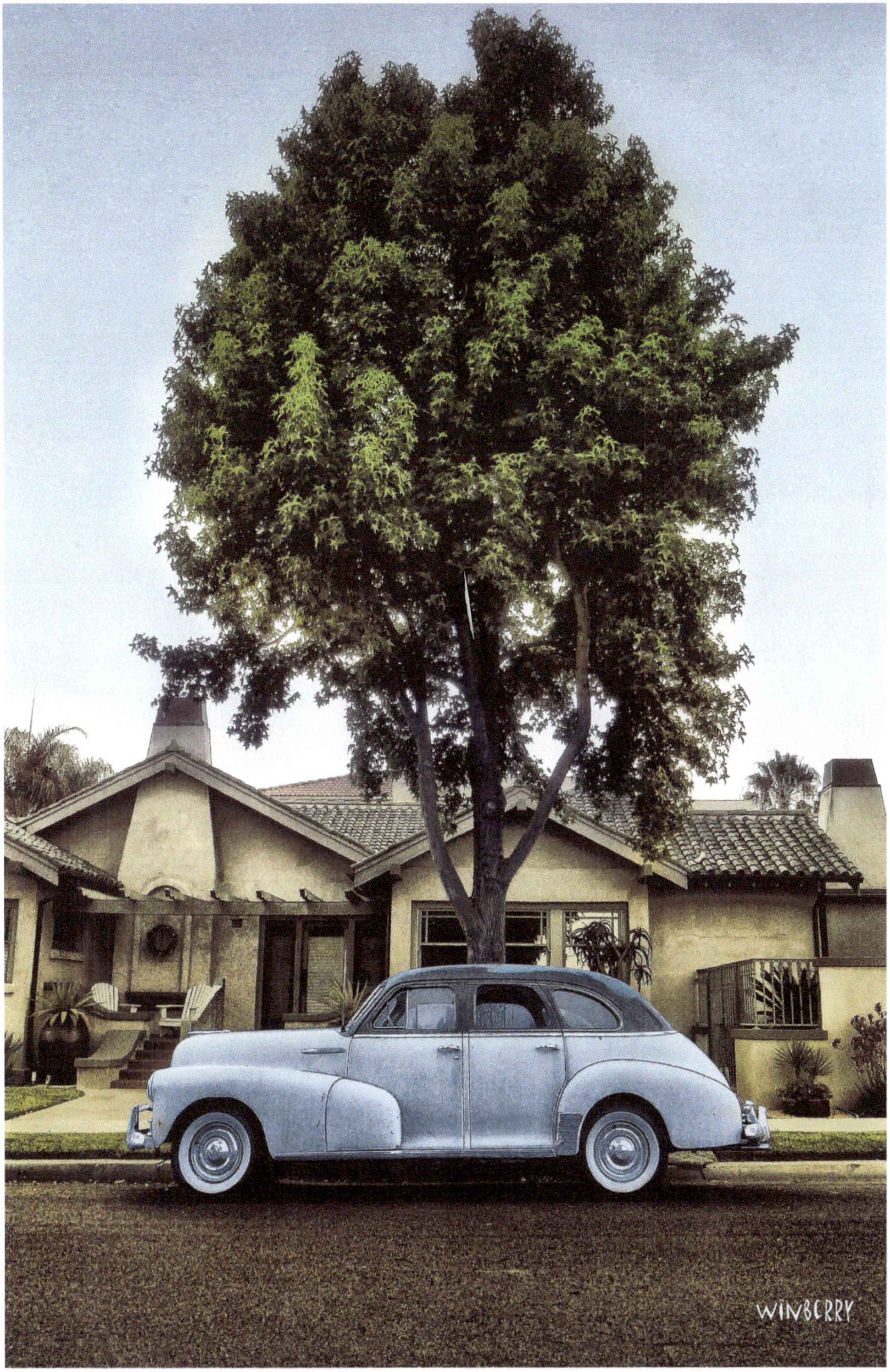
WINBERRY

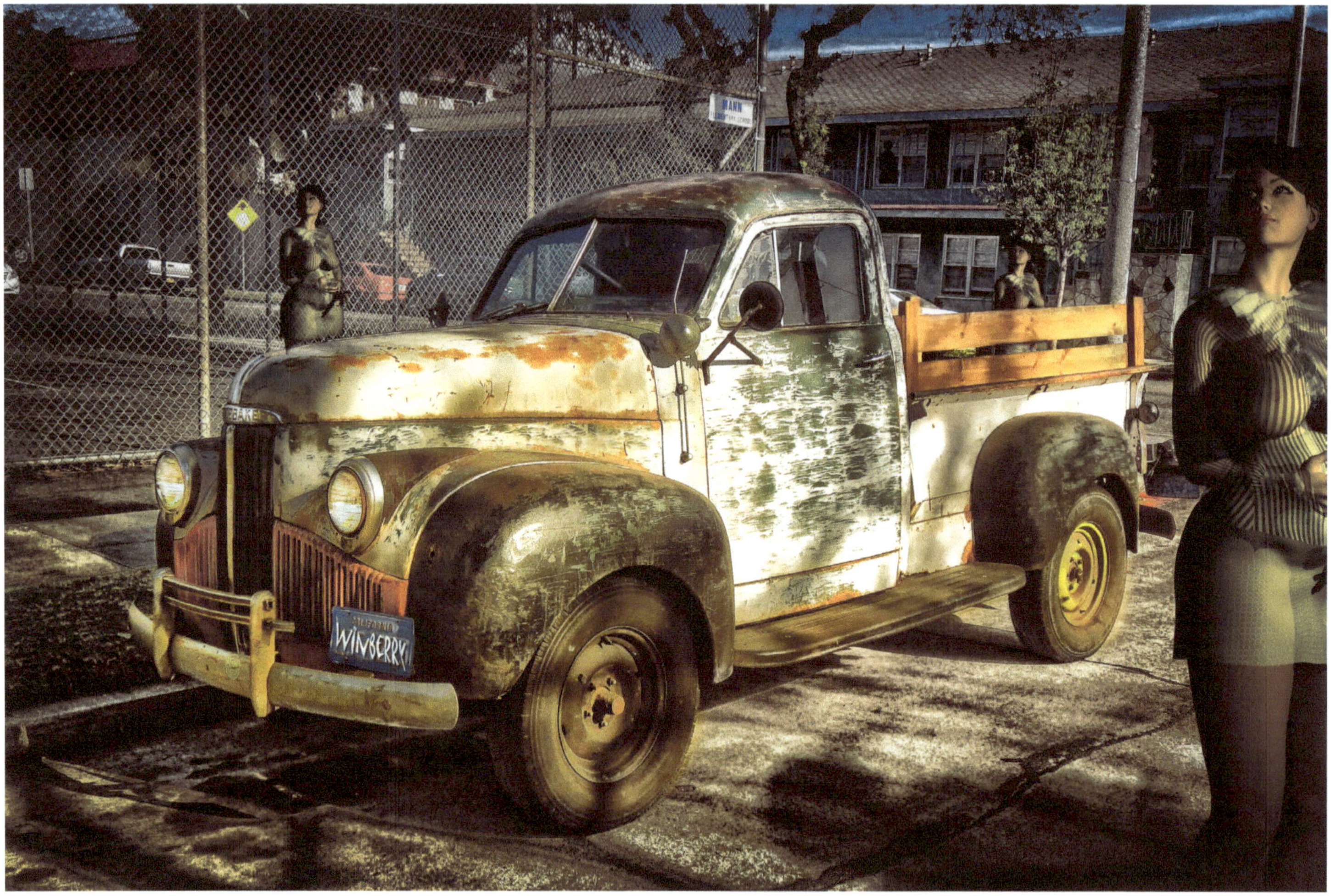
WINBERRY

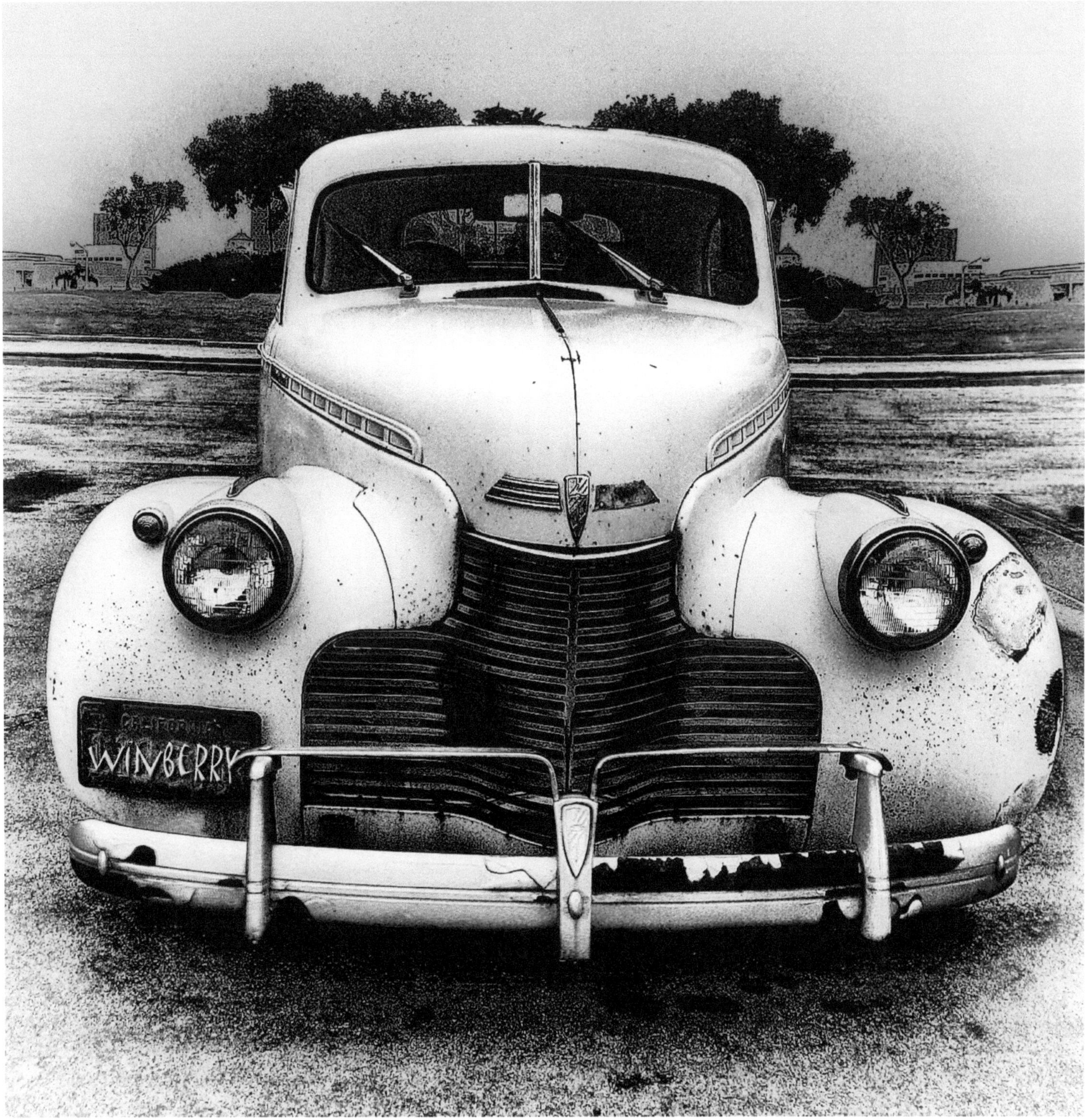
CALIFORNIA
WINBERRY

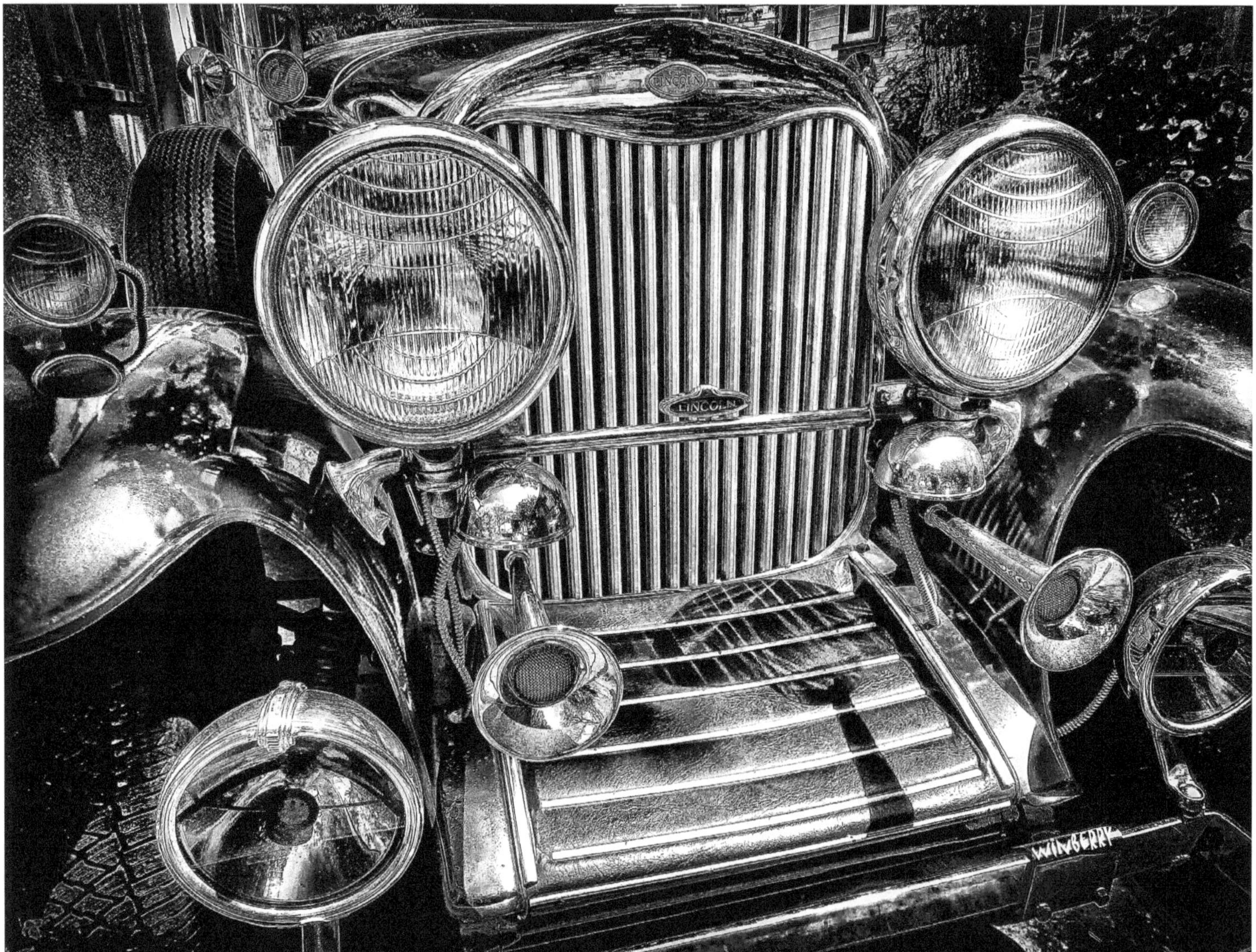
LINCOLN
LINCOLN
WINBERRY

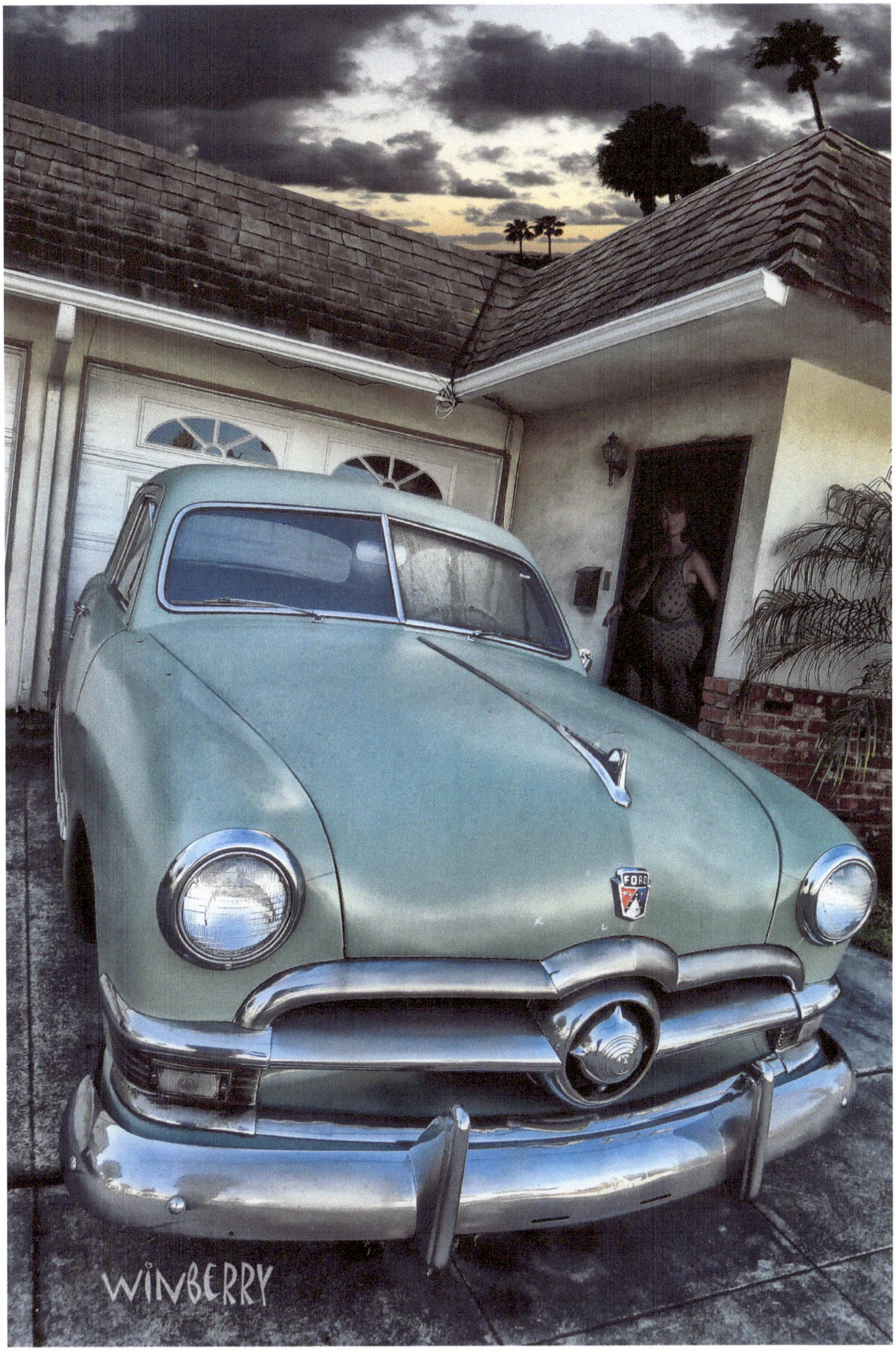
FORD
WINBERRY

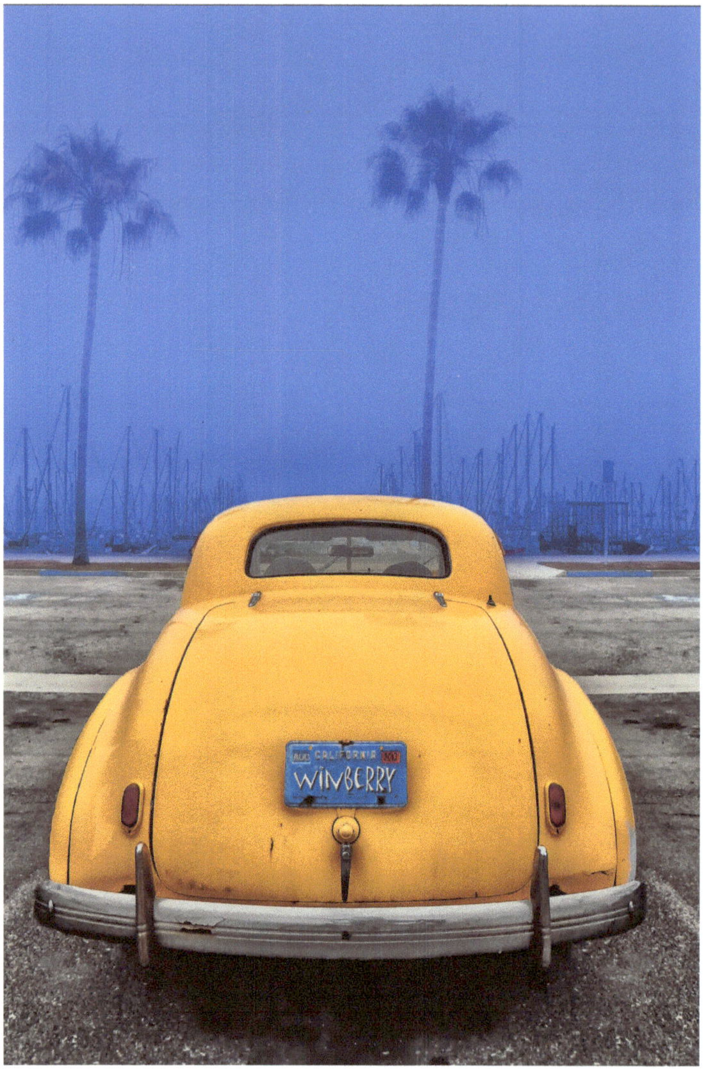
CALIFORNIA
WINBERRY
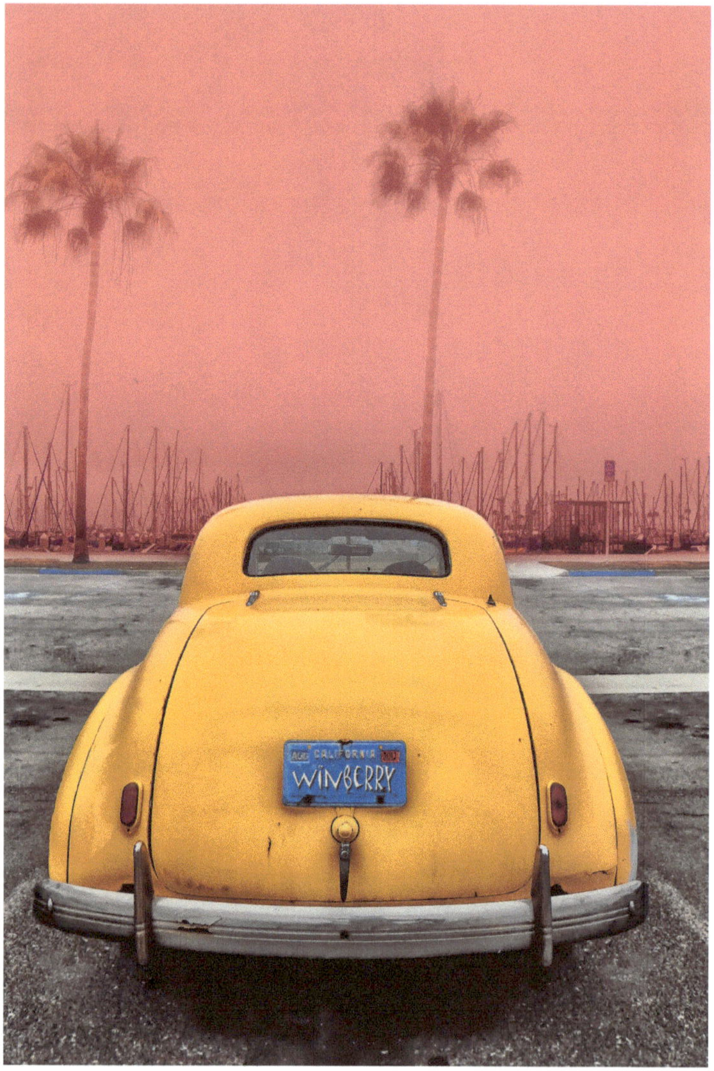
CALIFORNIA
WINBERRY

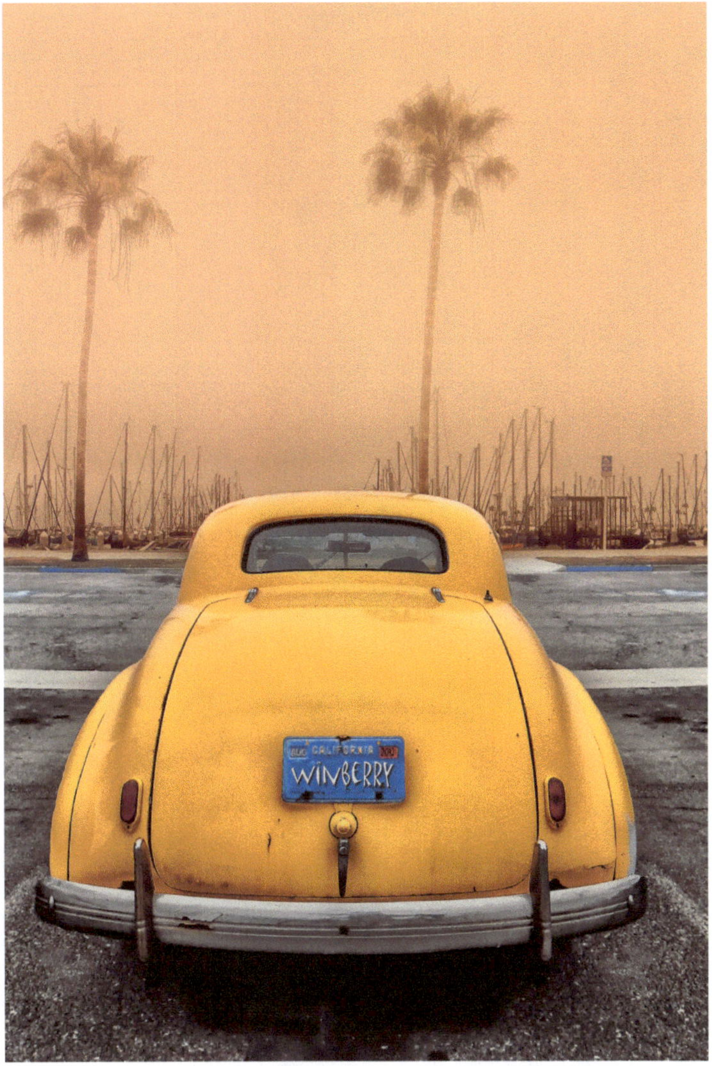
CALIFORNIA
WINBERRY

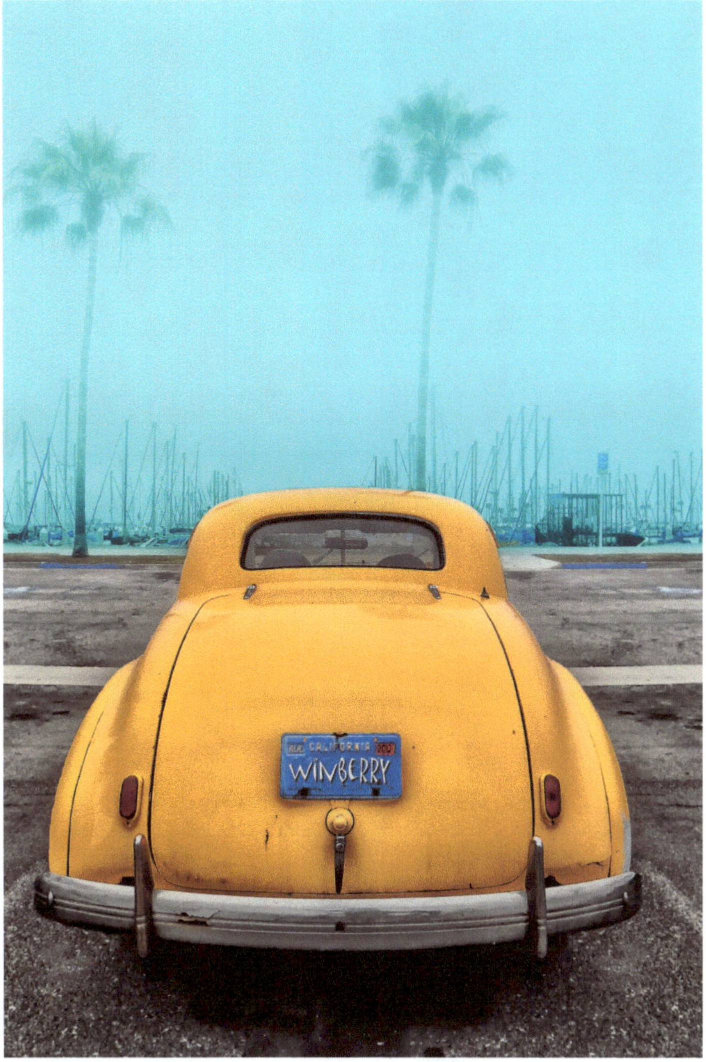
CALIFORNIA
WINBERRY

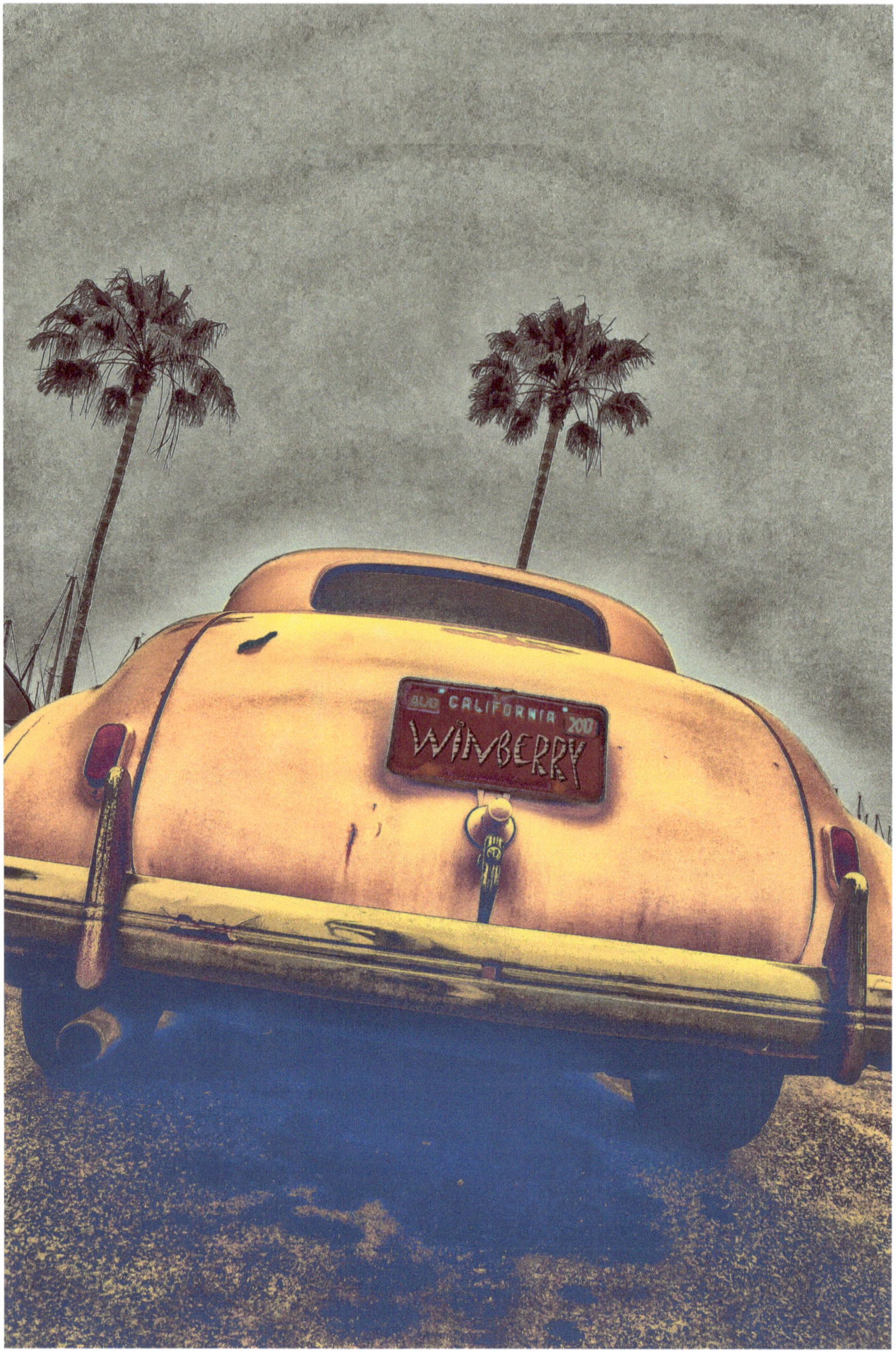
CALIFORNIA
2013
WINBERRY

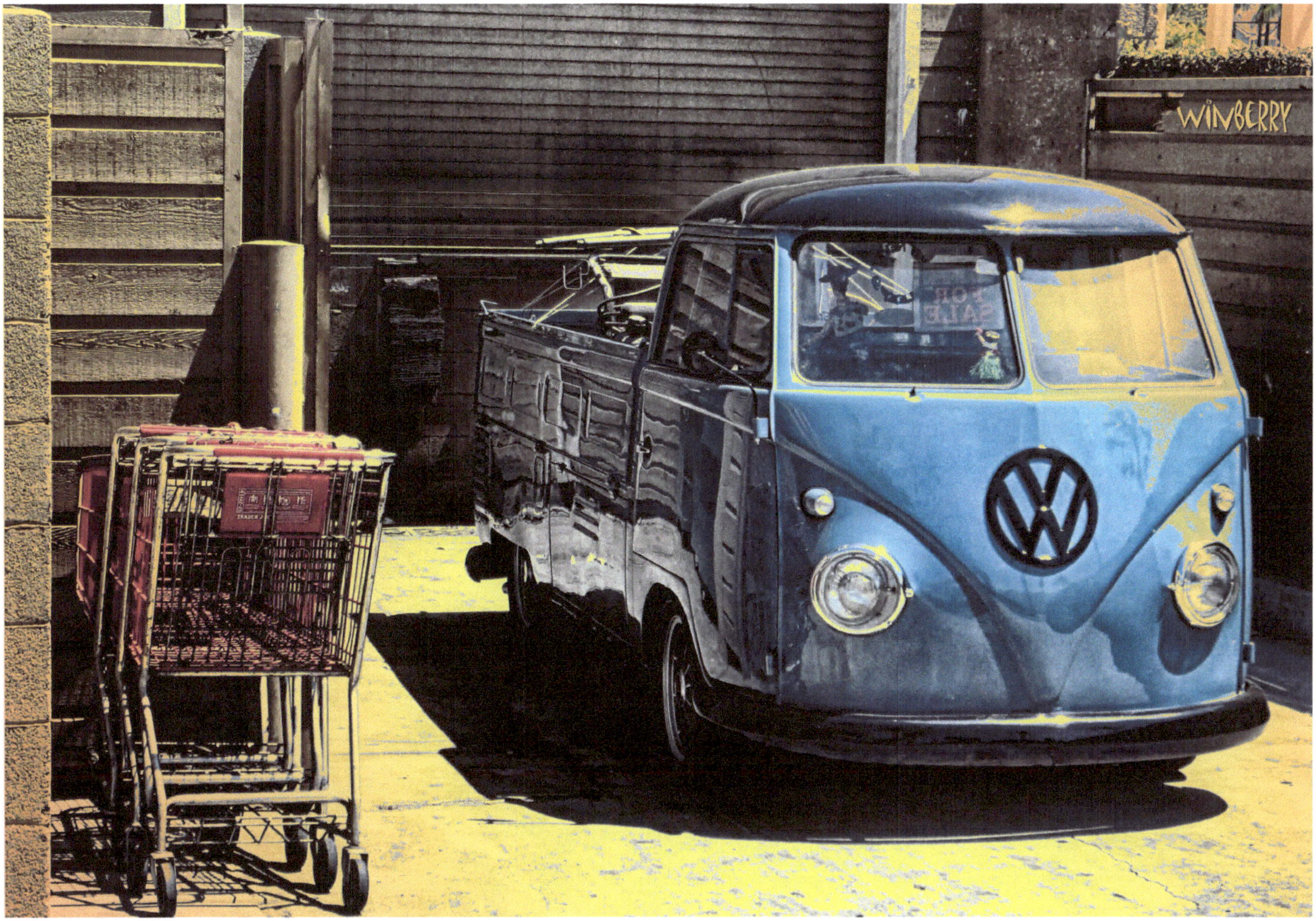
WINBERRY

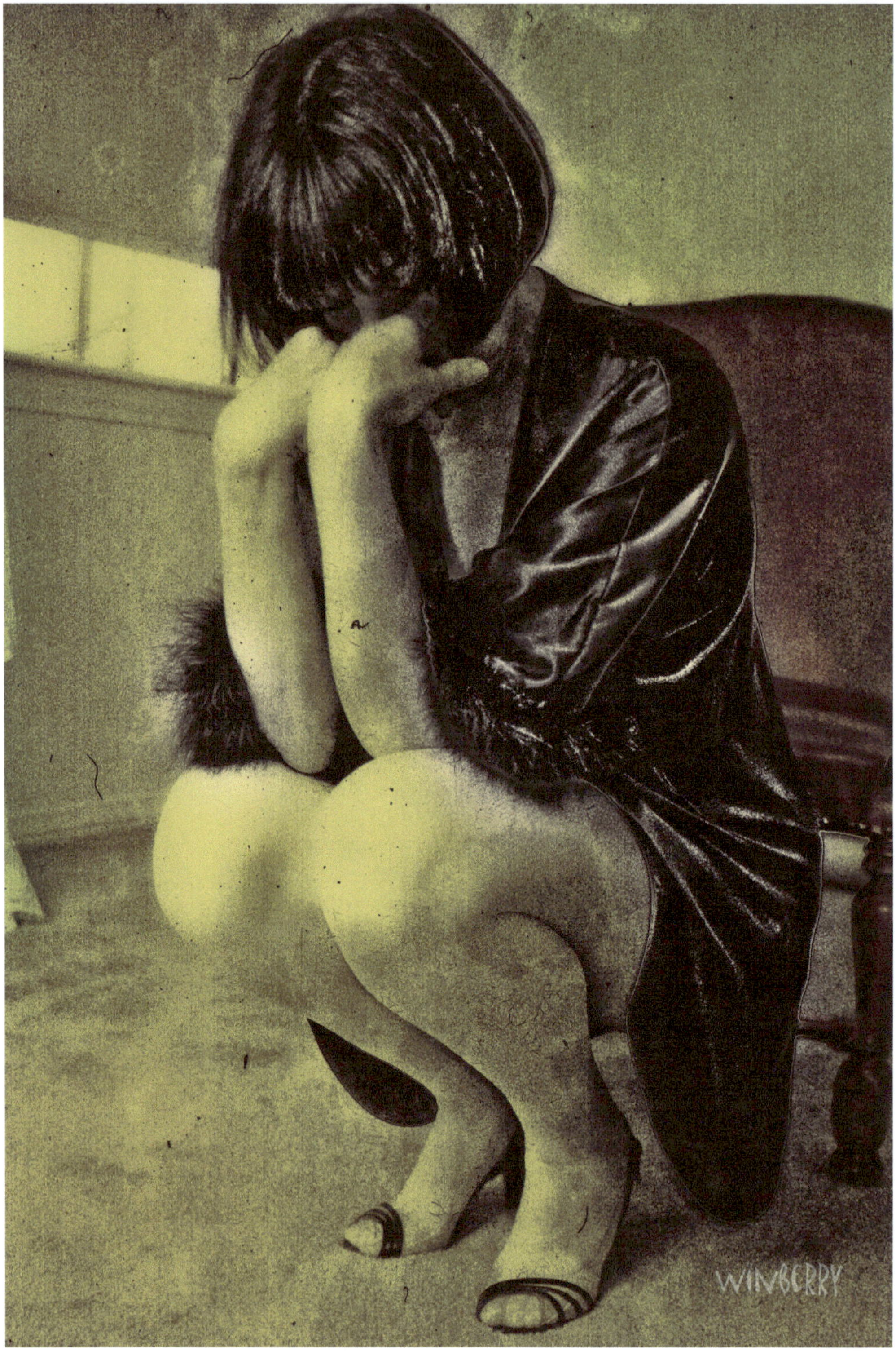
WINBERRY

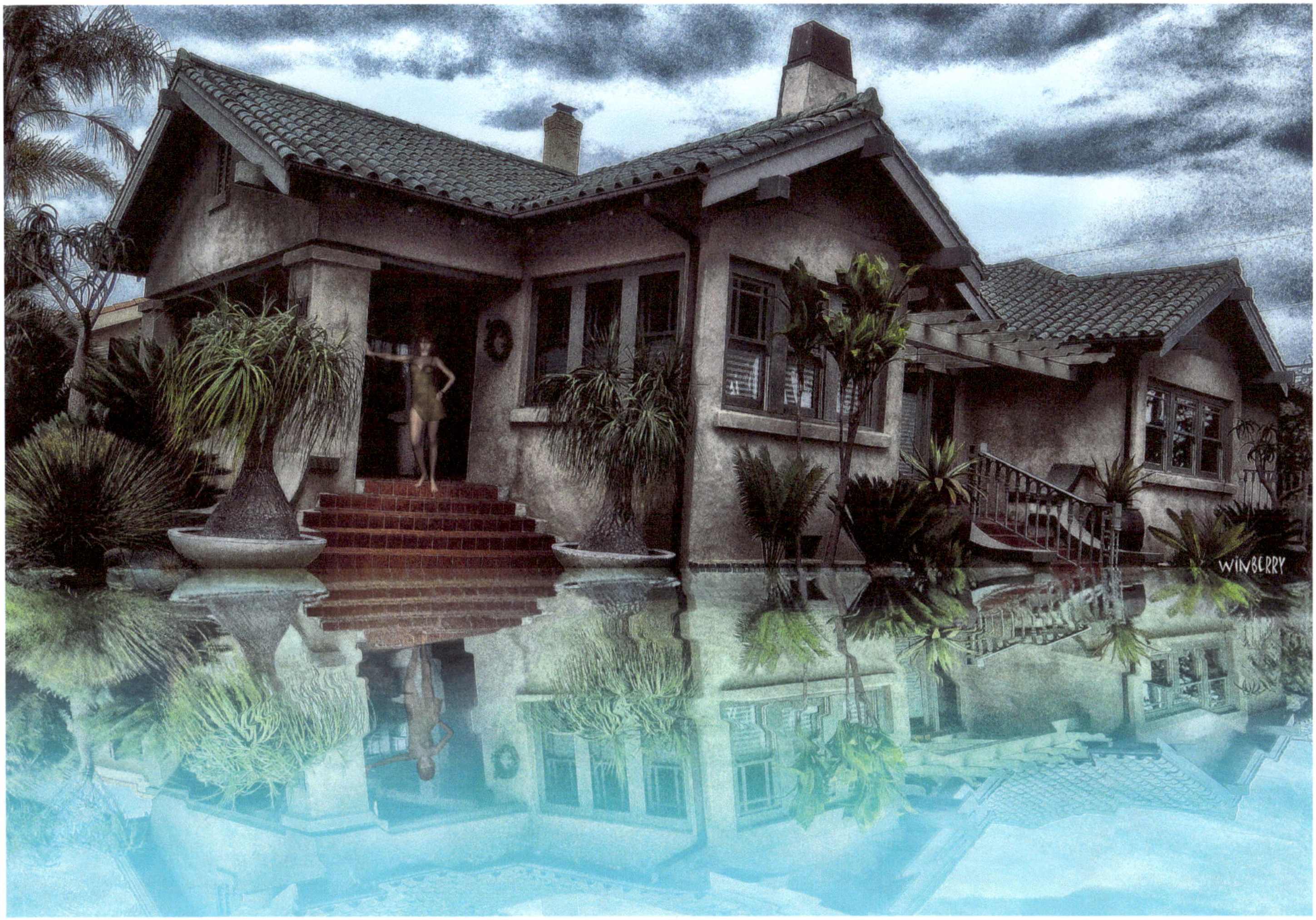
WINBERRY

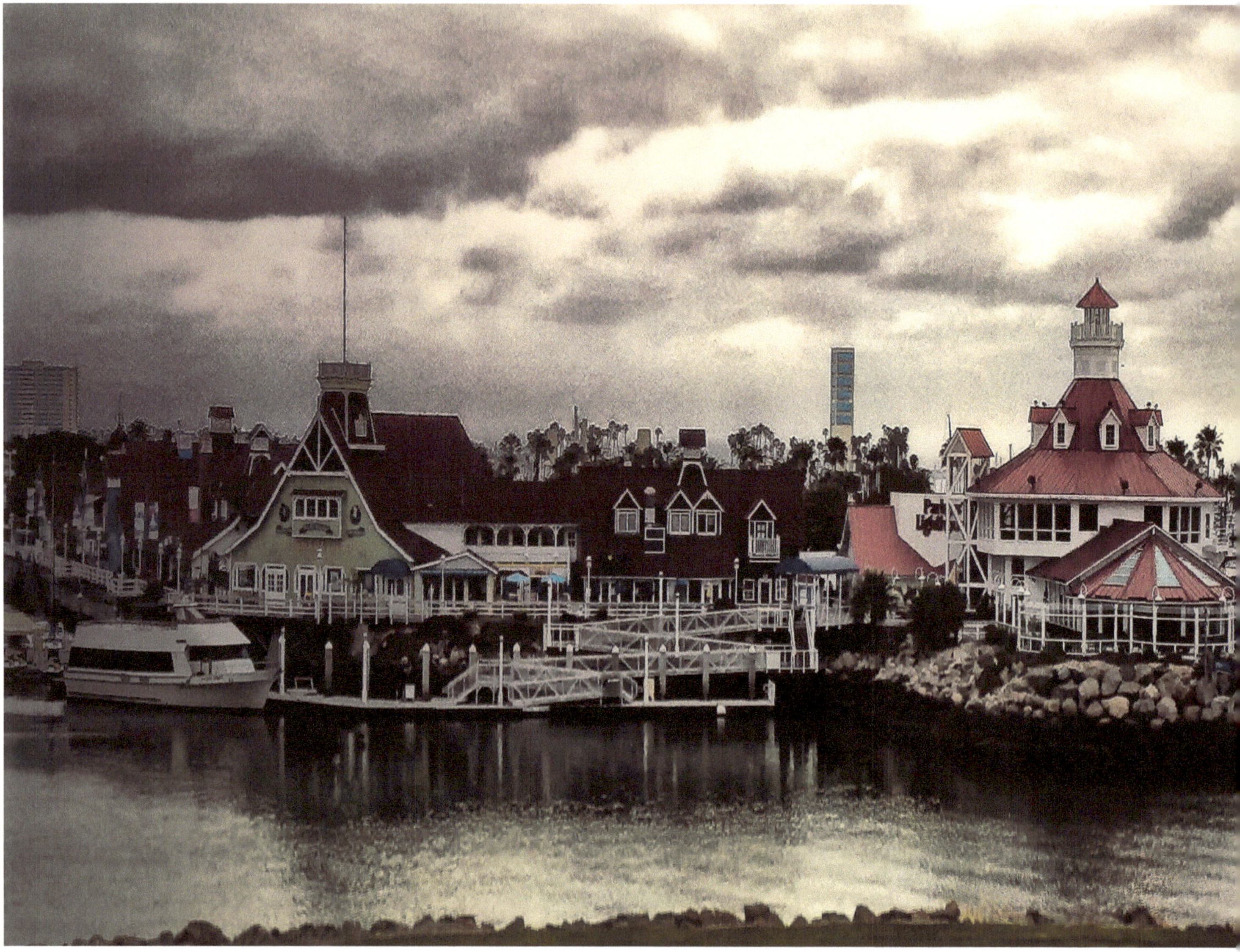

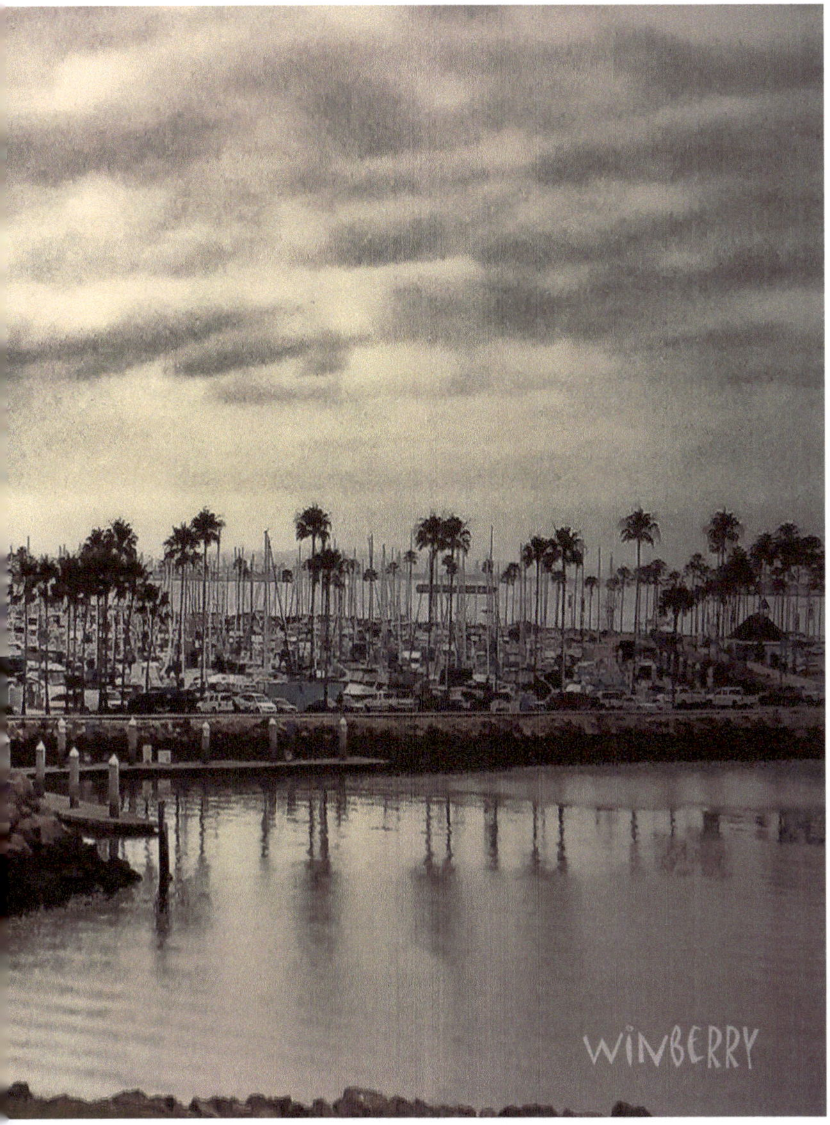
WINBERRY

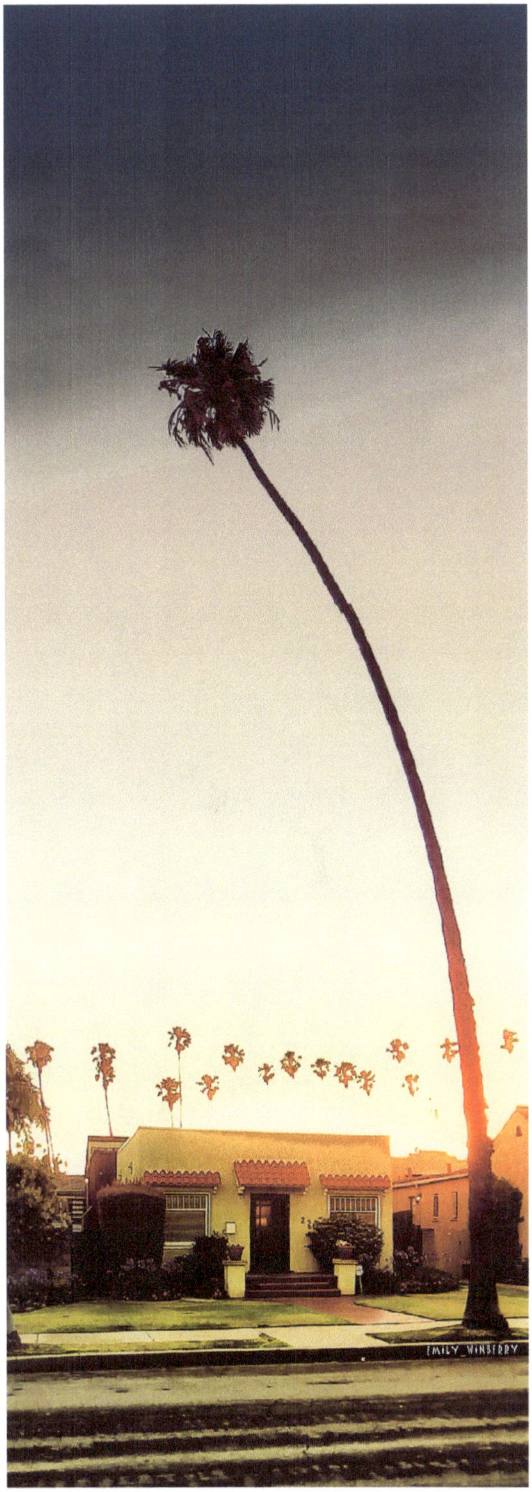
EMILY WINBERRY

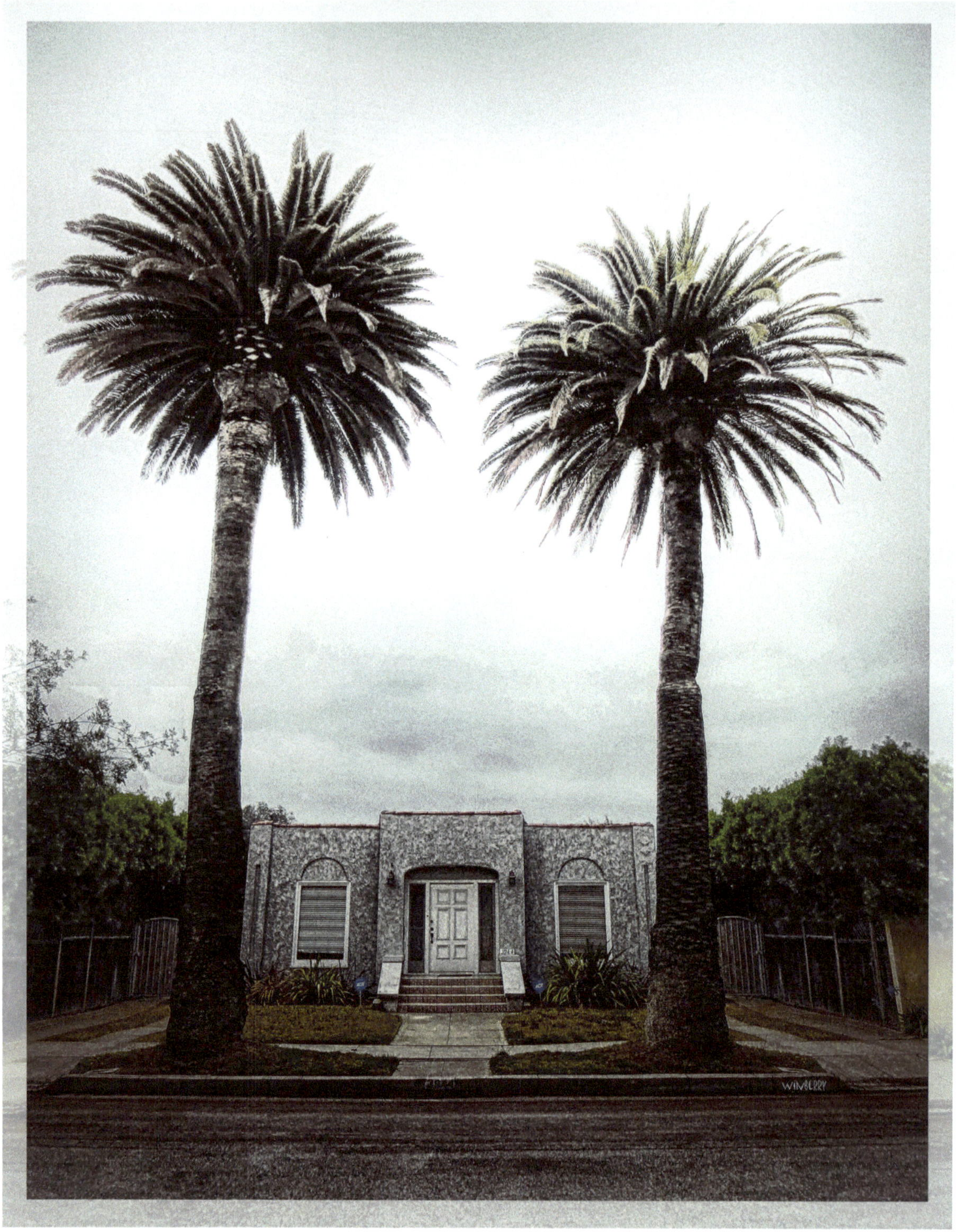
WINBERRY

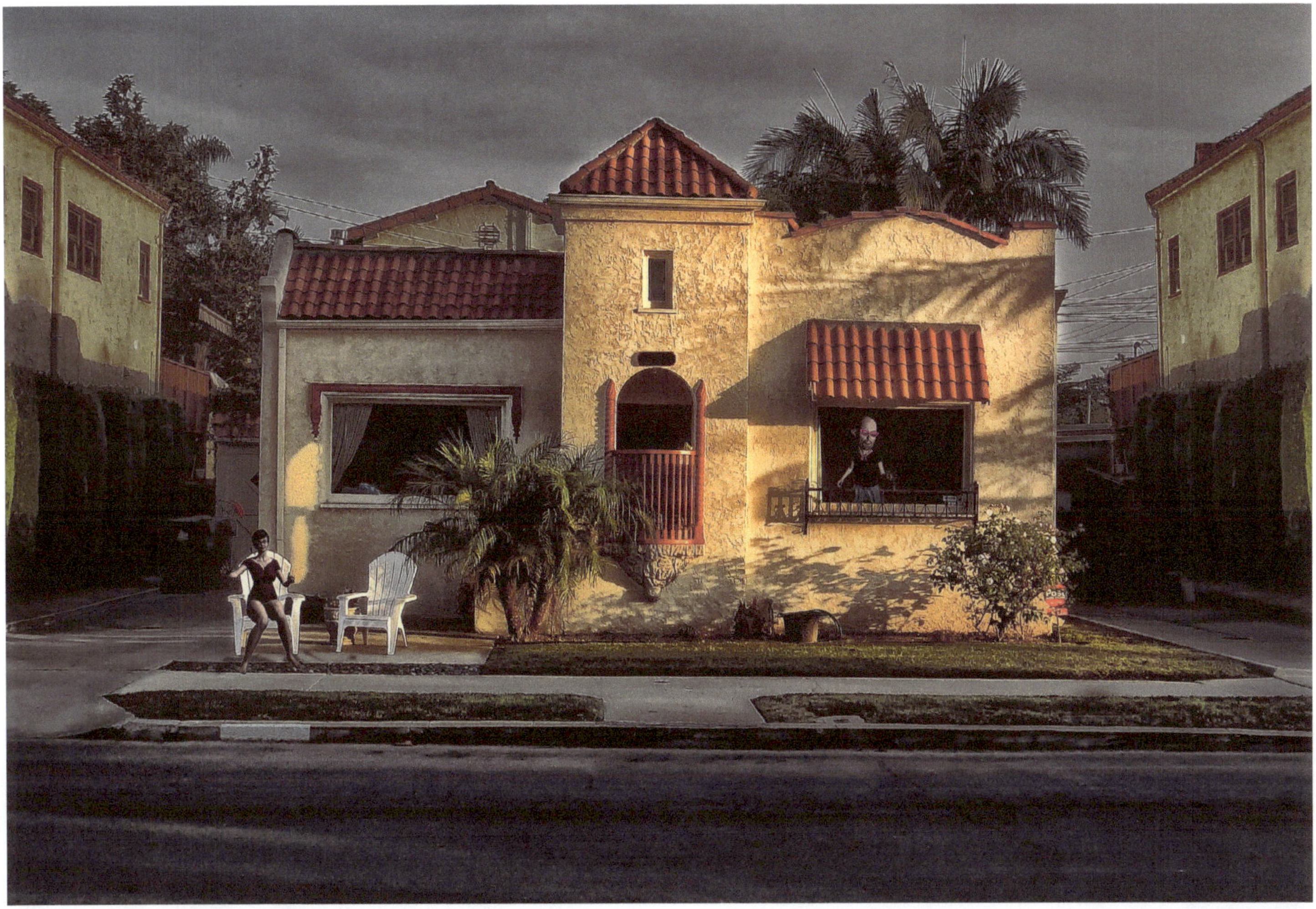

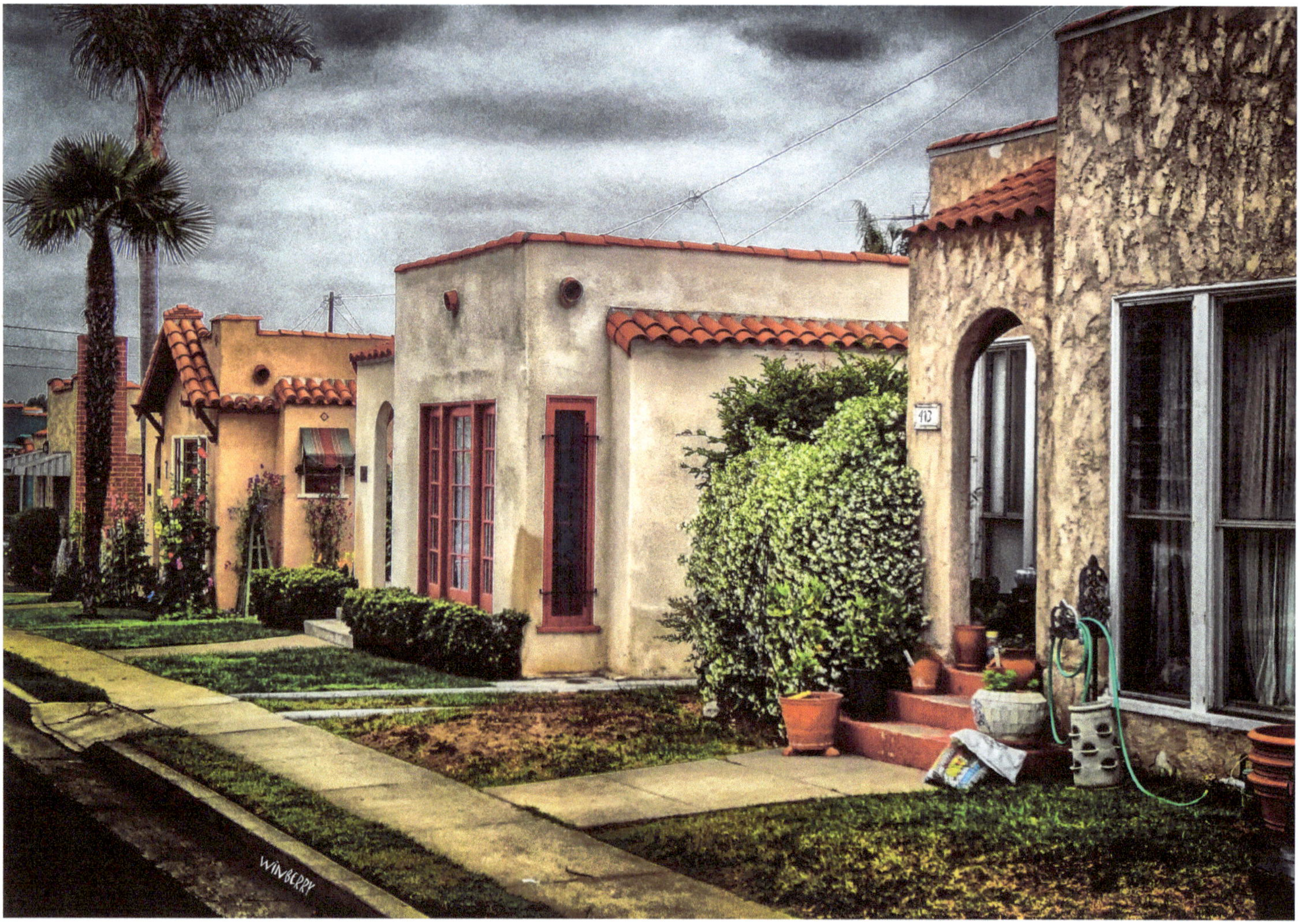
WINBERRY

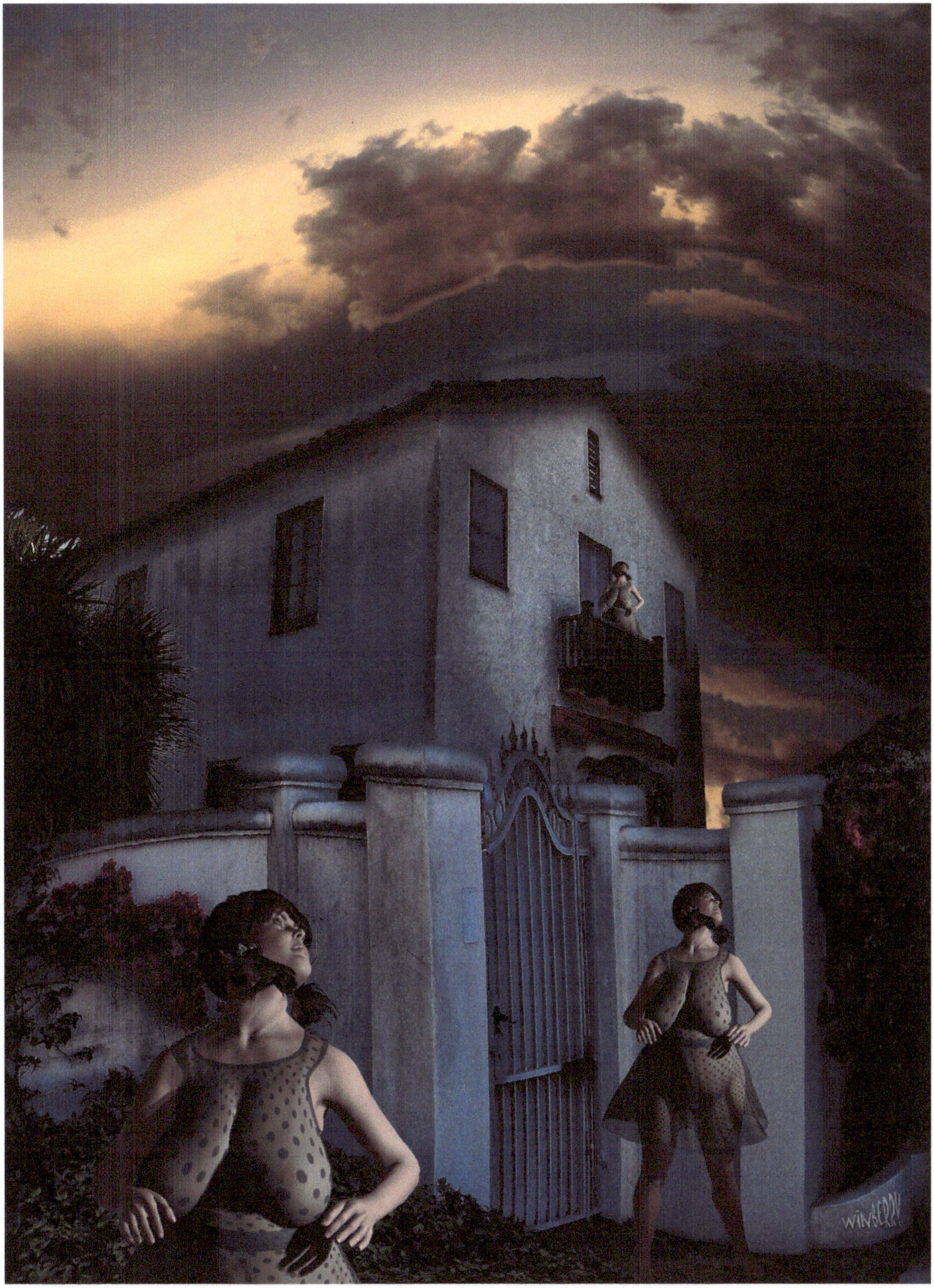
WINBERRY

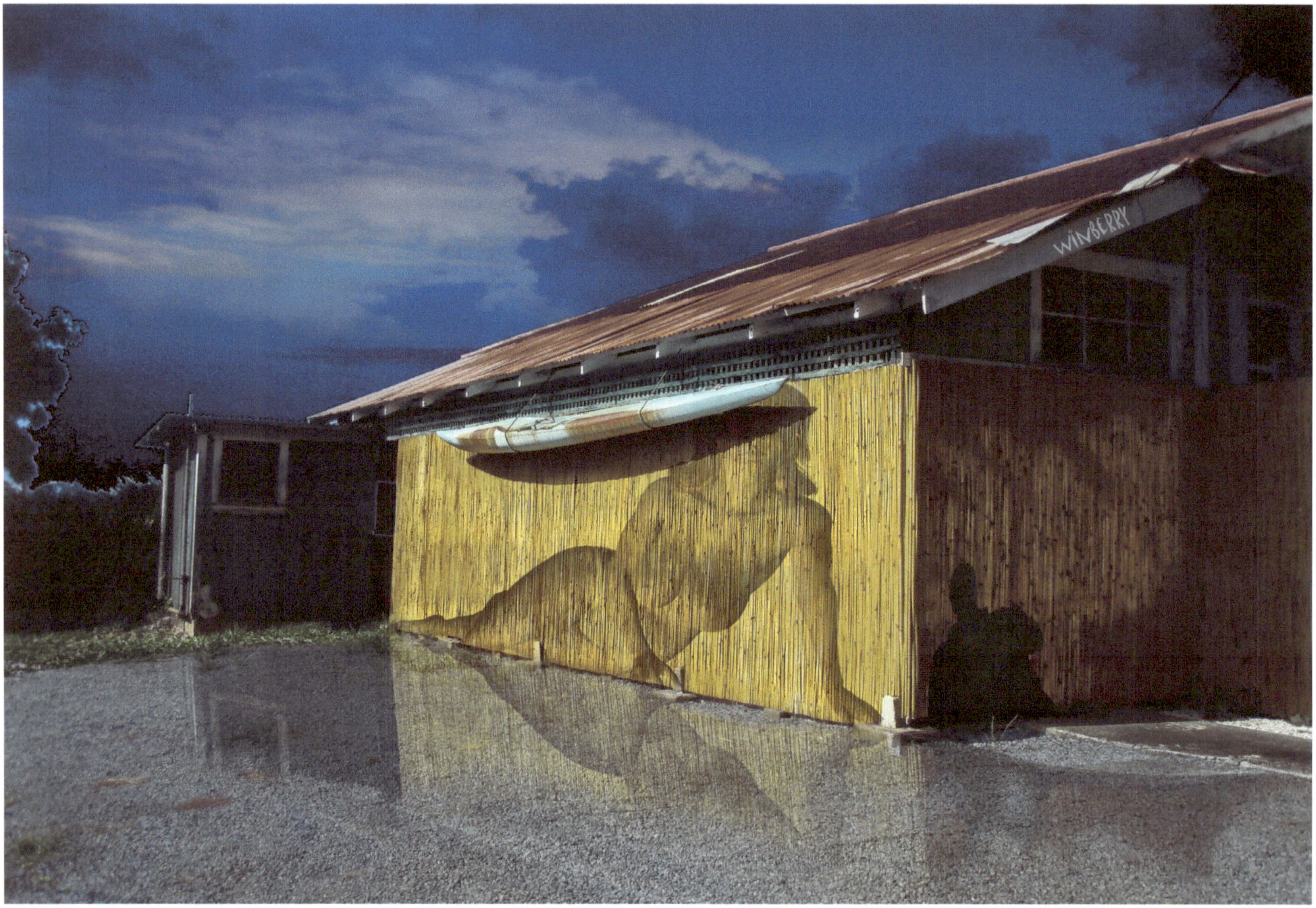
WINBERRY

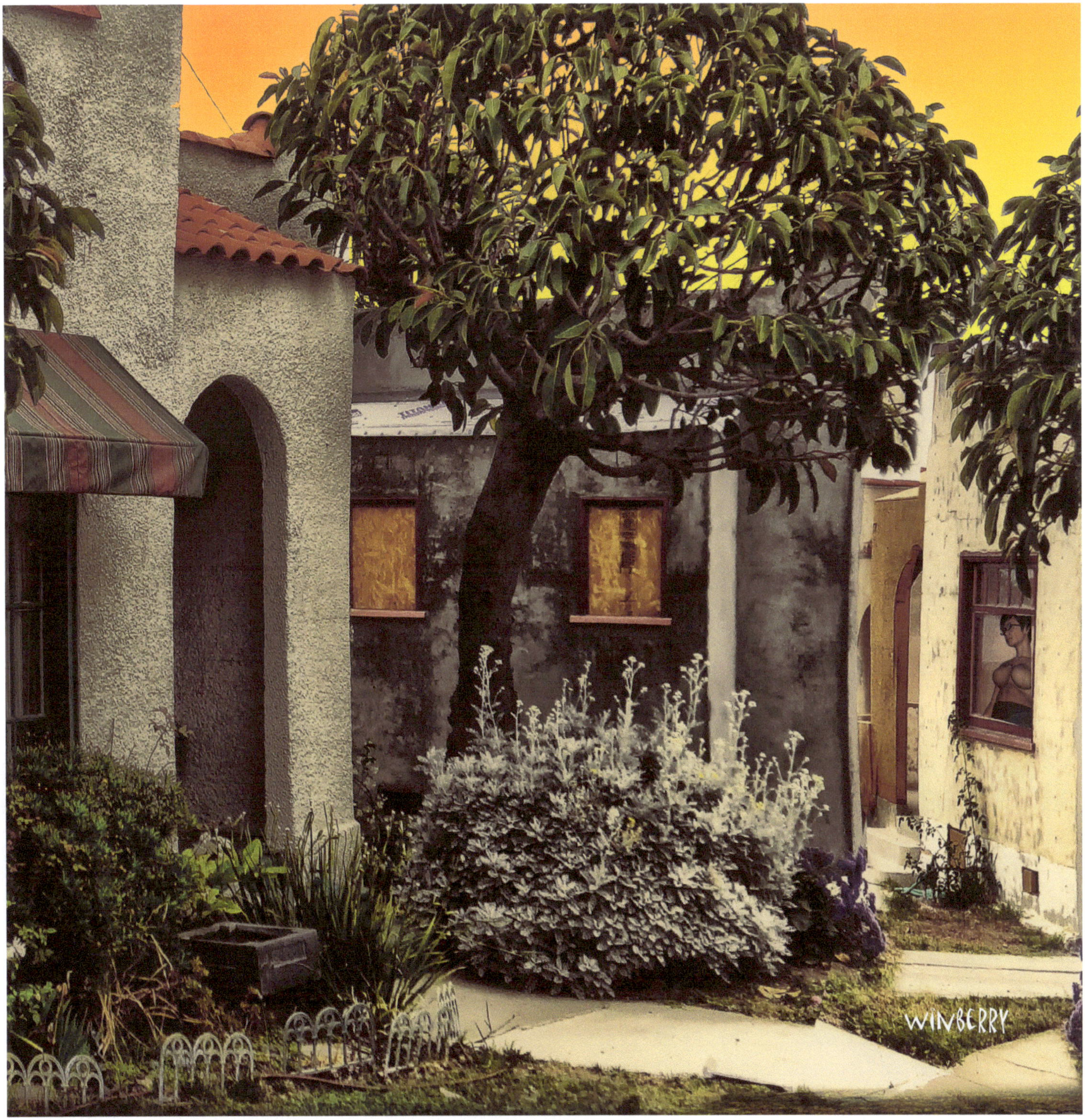
WINBERRY

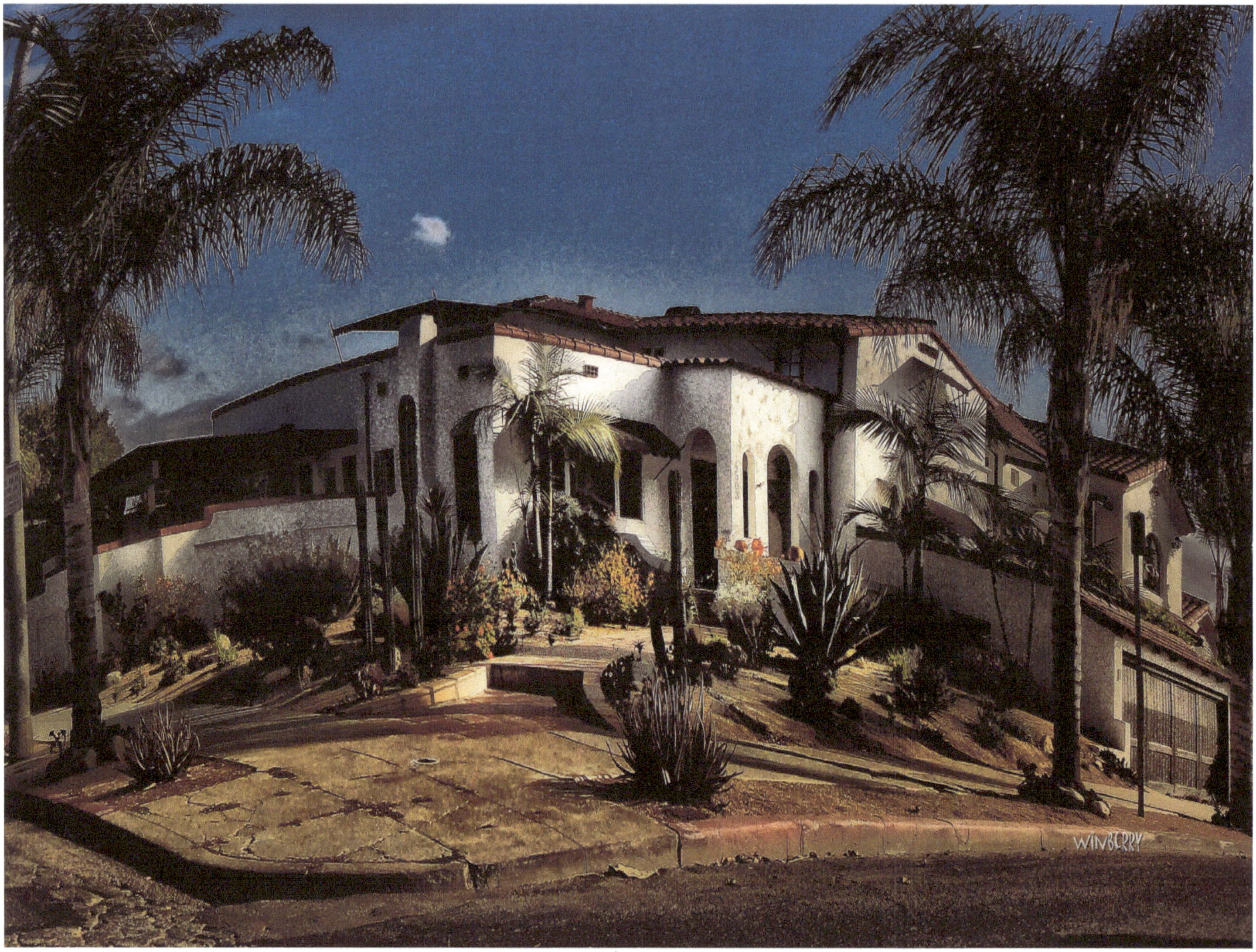
WINBERRY

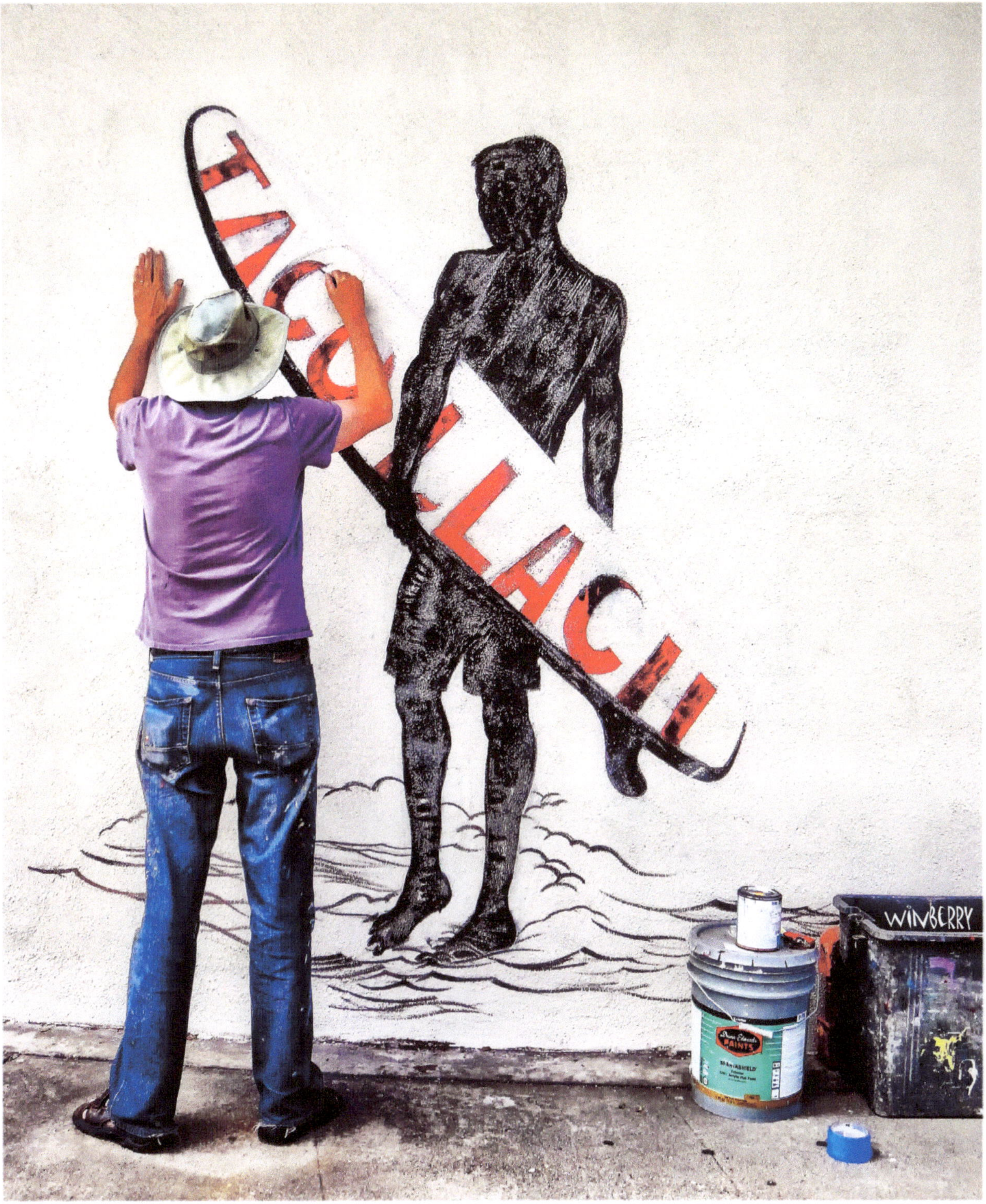
WINBERRY

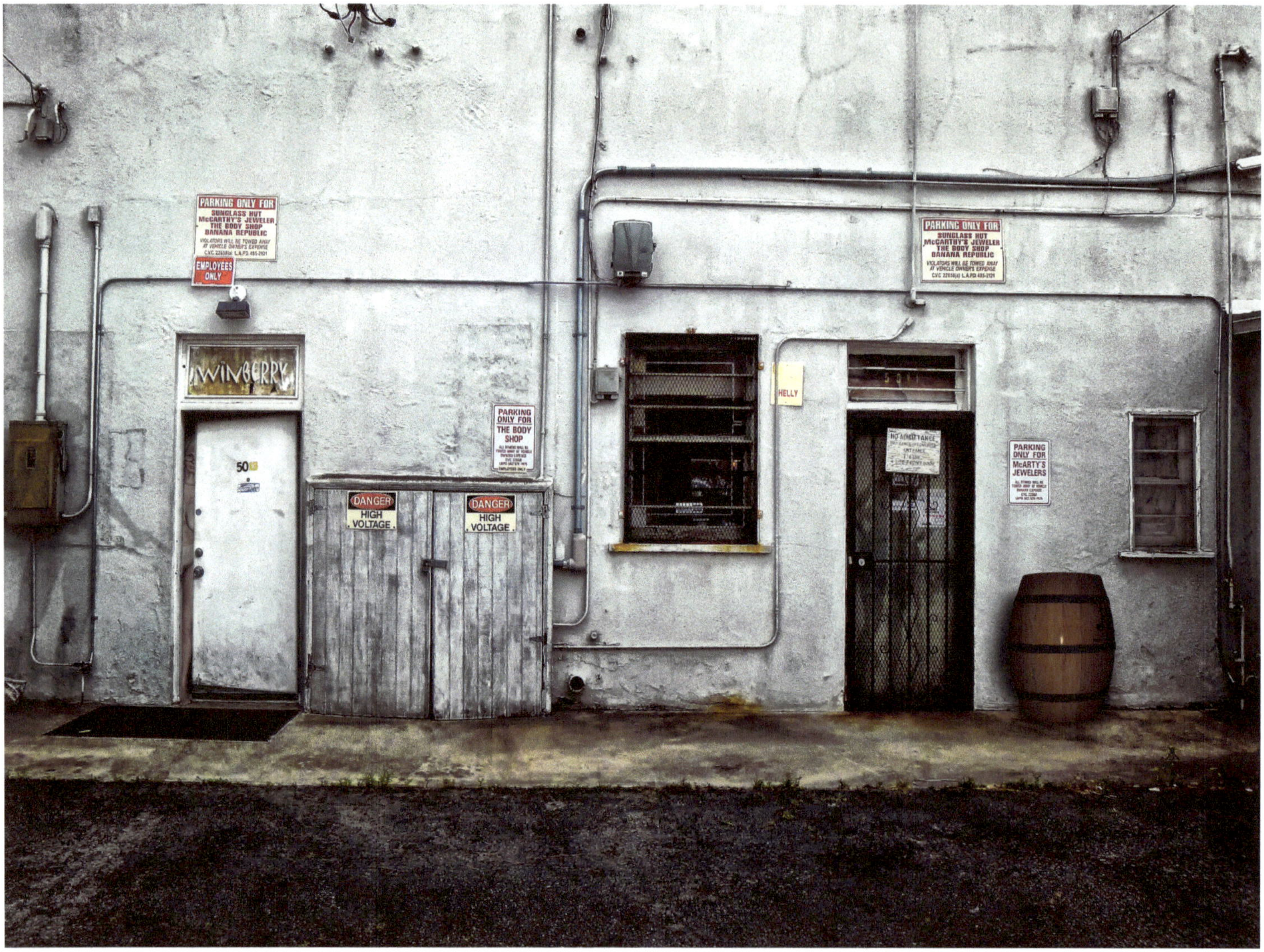
PARKING ONLY FOR
SUNGLASS HUT
McCARTHY'S JEWELER
THE BODY SHOP
BANANA REPUBLIC
VIOLATORS WILL BE TOWED AWAY AT VEHICLE OWNER'S EXPENSE
EMPLOYEES ONLY
WINBERRY
50
PARKING ONLY FOR
THE BODY SHOP
DANGER
HIGH VOLTAGE
DANGER
HIGH VOLTAGE
HELLY
PARKING ONLY FOR
SUNGLASS HUT
McCARTHY'S JEWELER
THE BODY SHOP
BANANA REPUBLIC
VIOLATORS WILL BE TOWED AWAY AT VEHICLE OWNER'S EXPENSE
PARKING ONLY FOR
McARTY'S JEWELERS

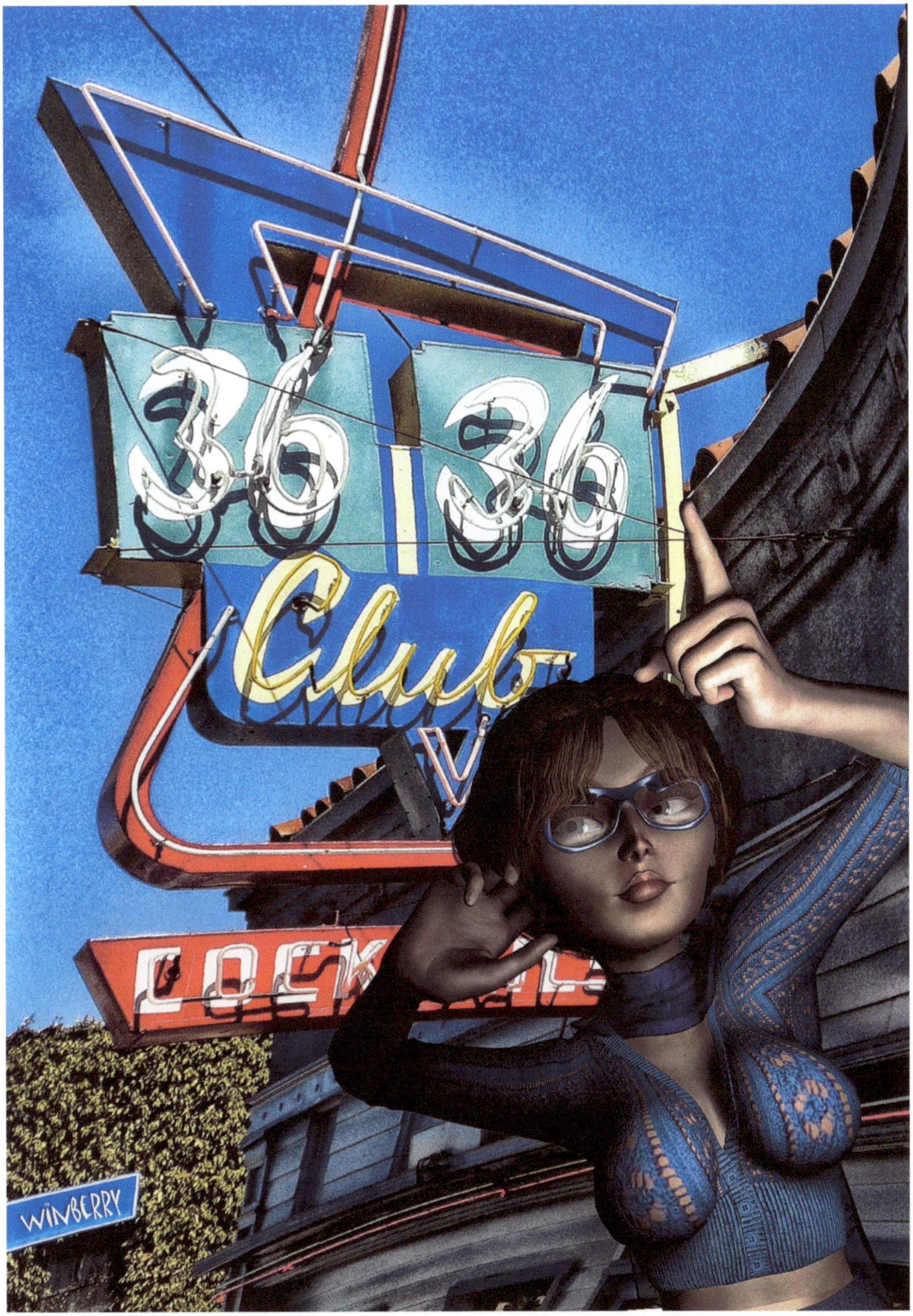
36
36
Club
WINBERRY

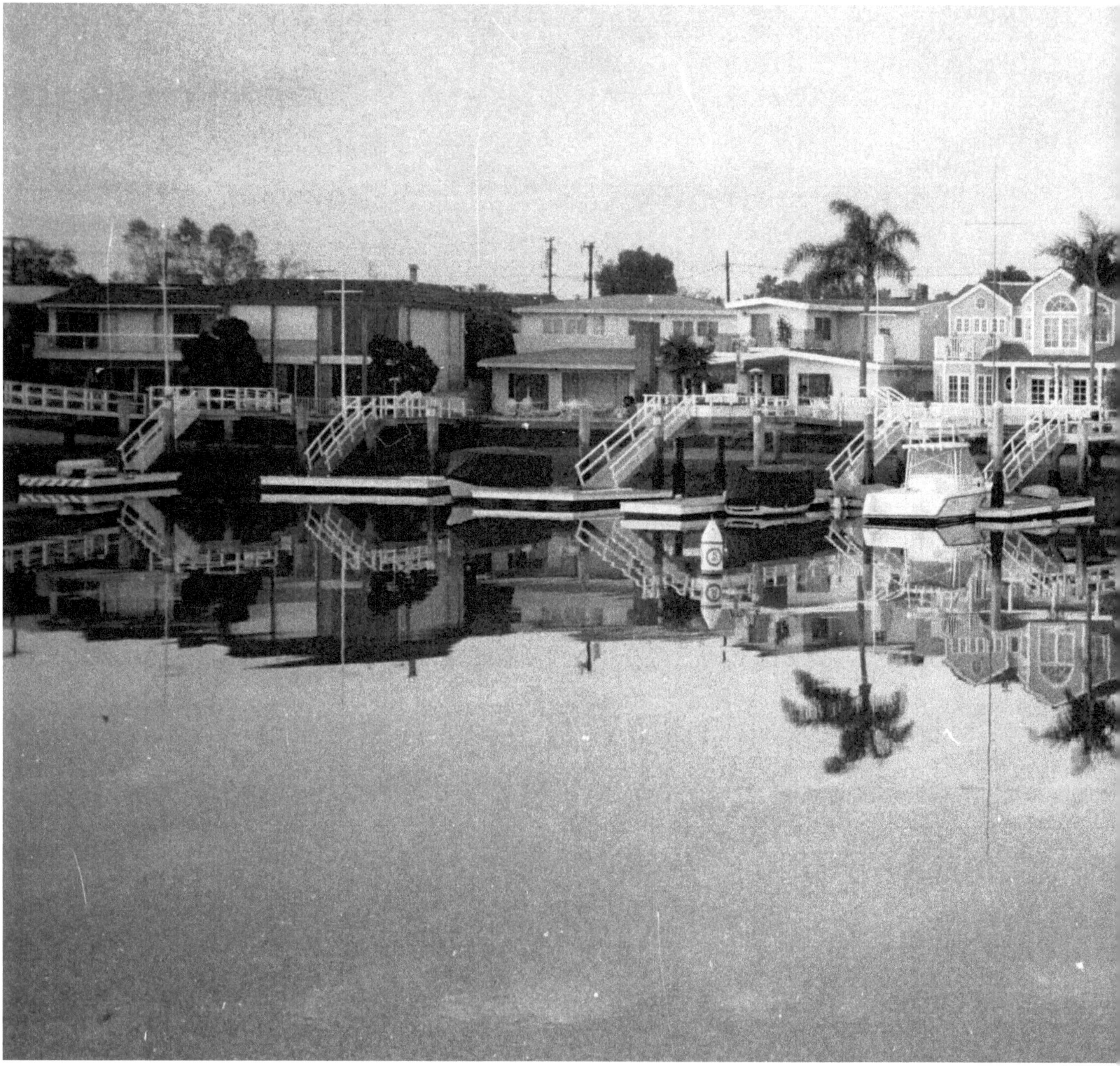

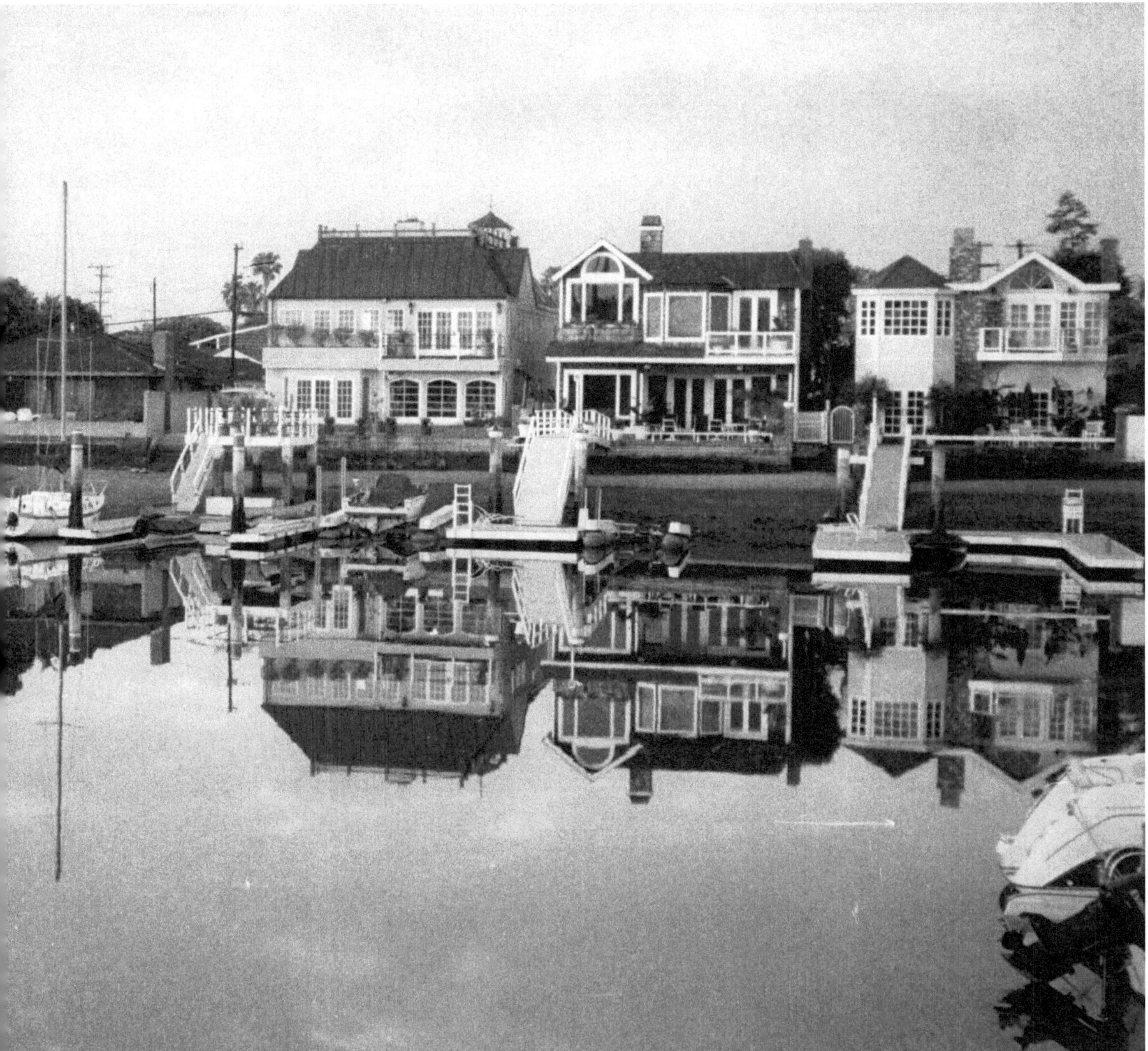

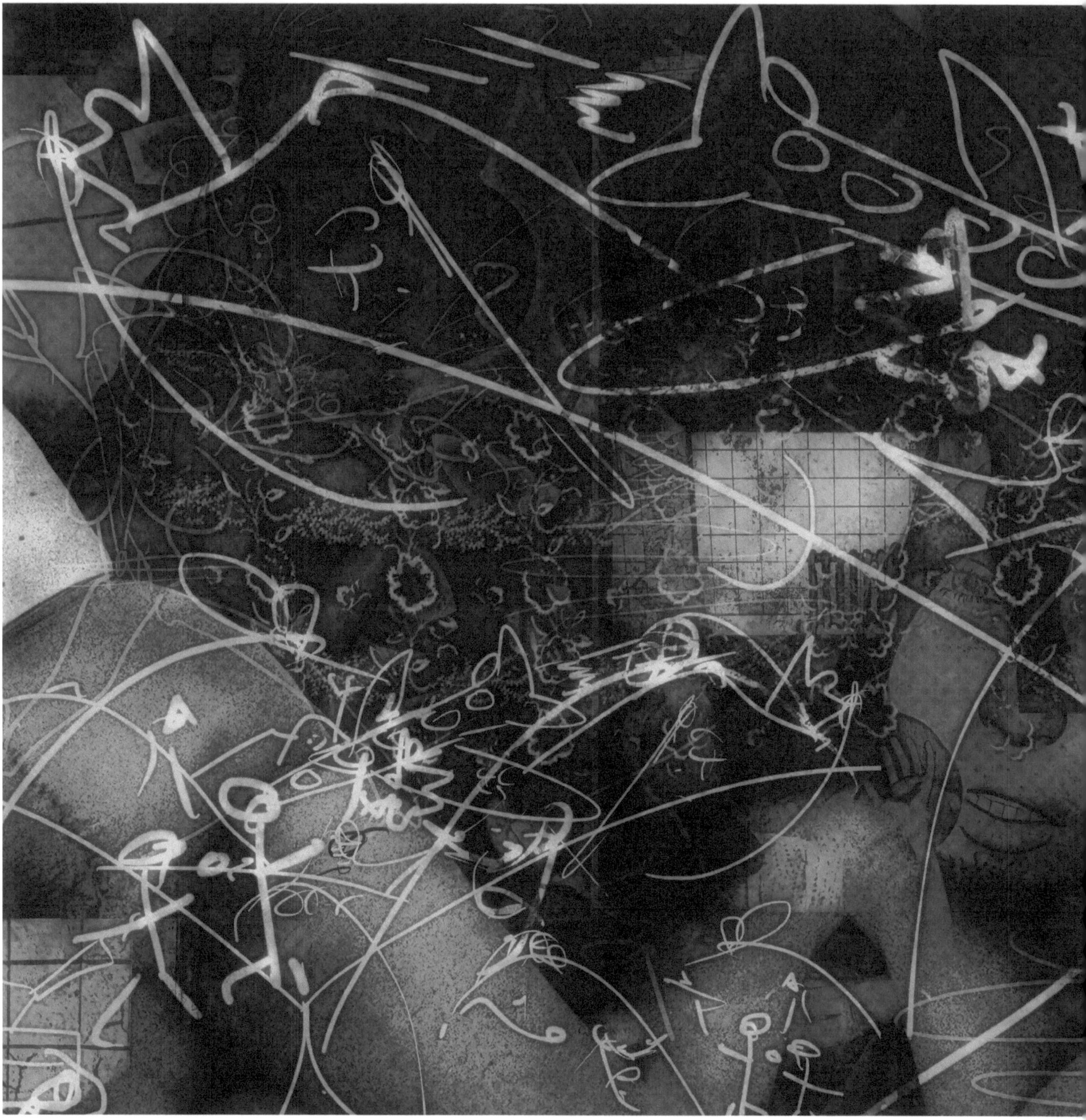

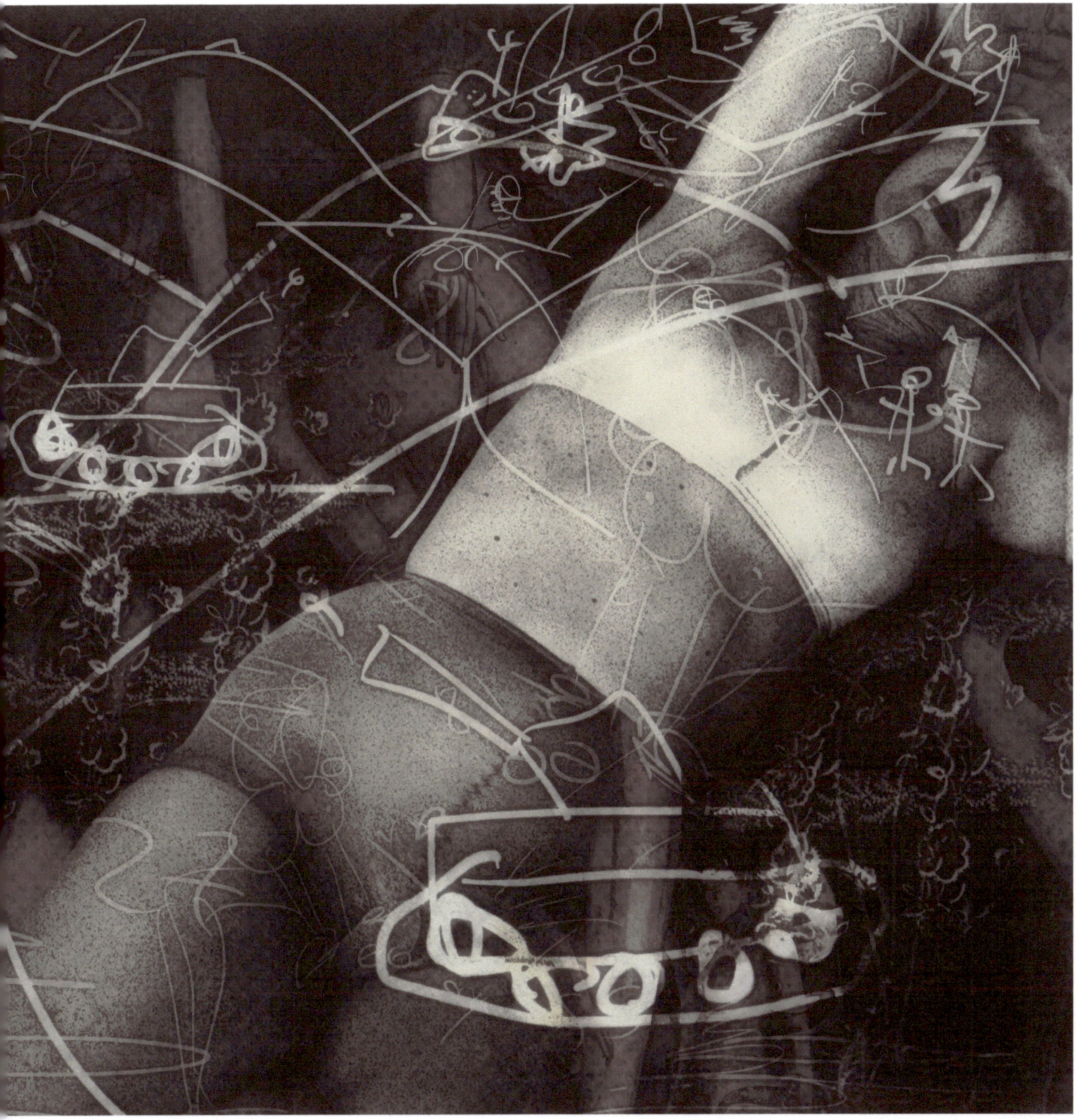

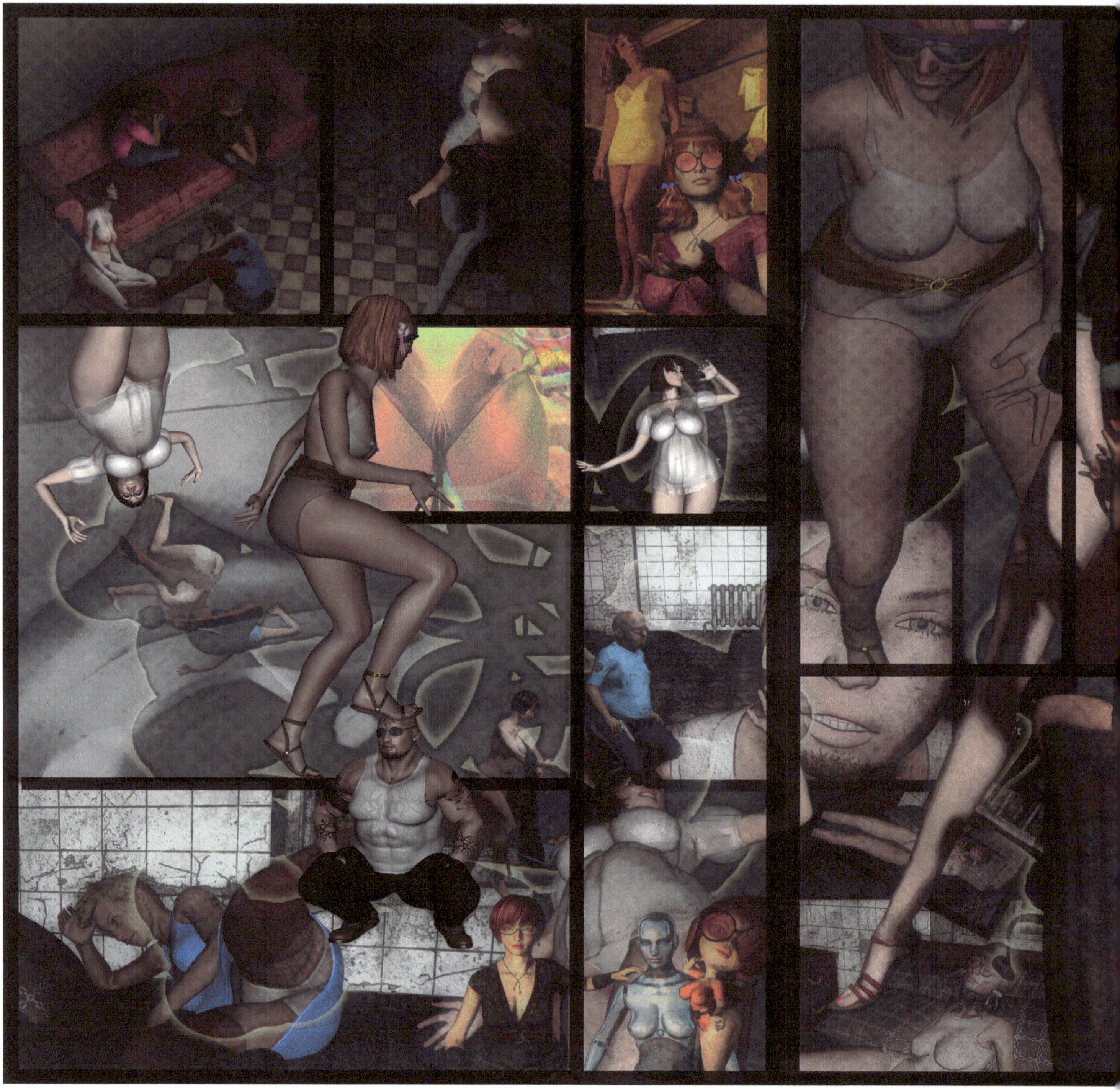

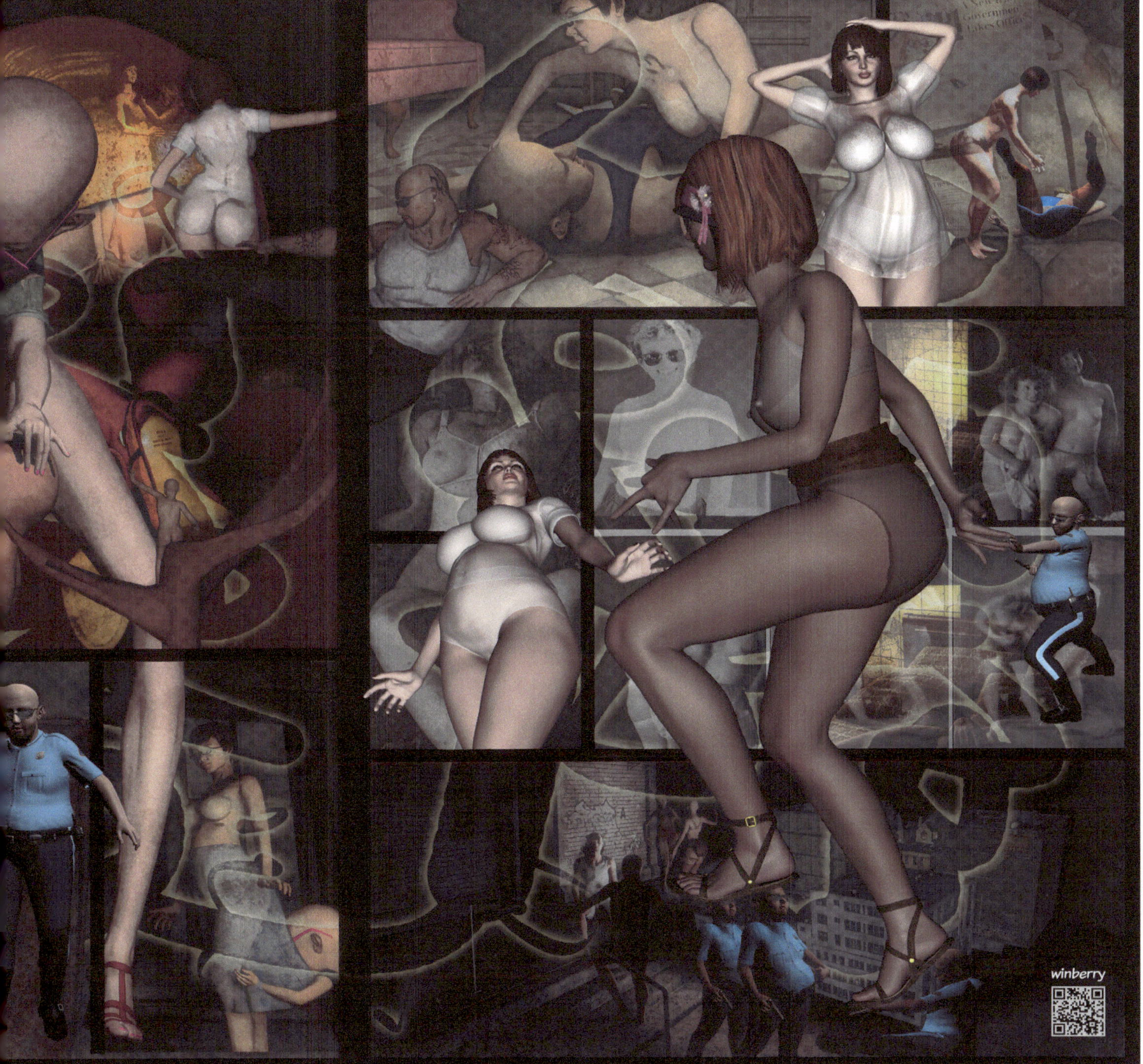
winberry

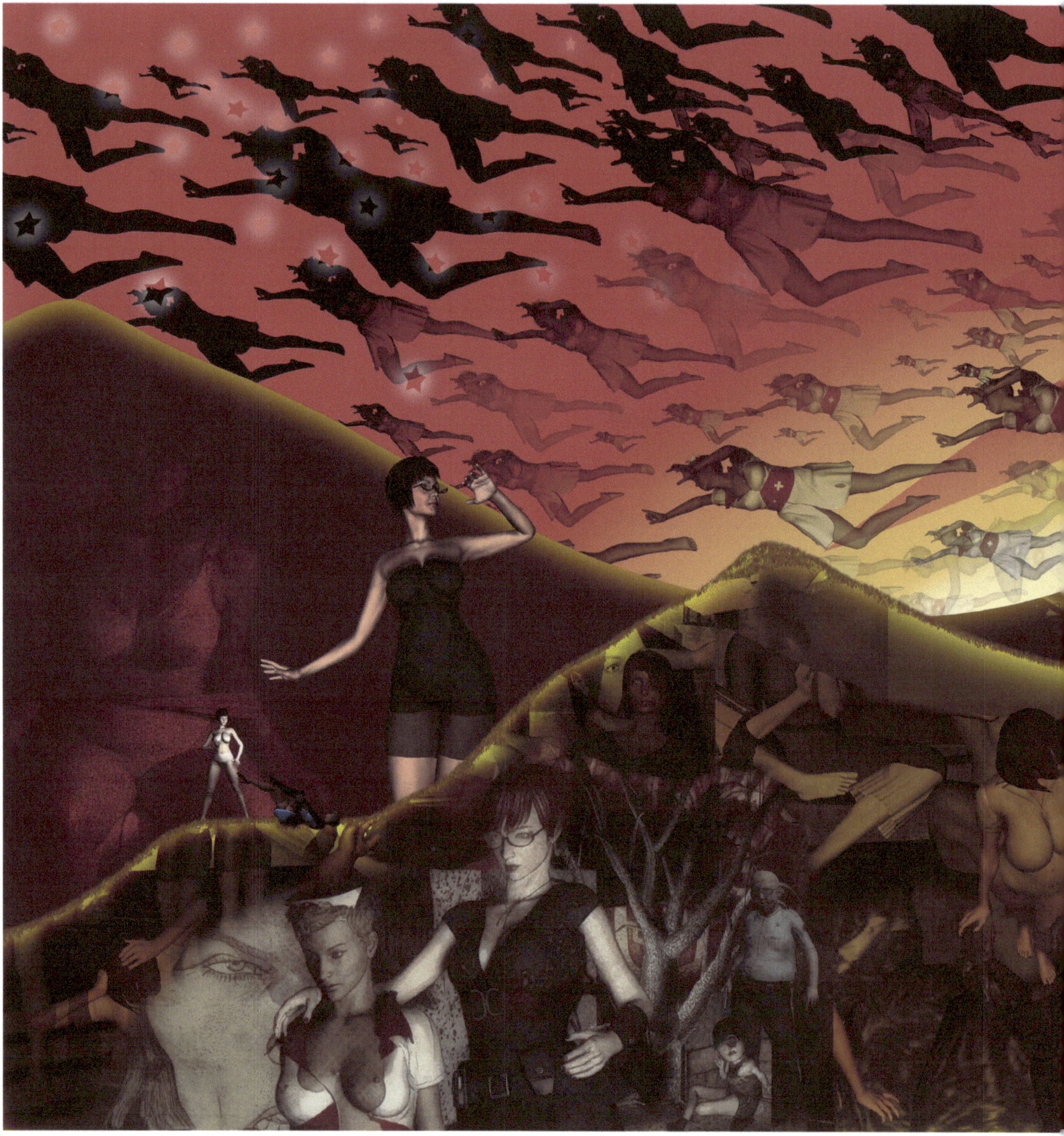

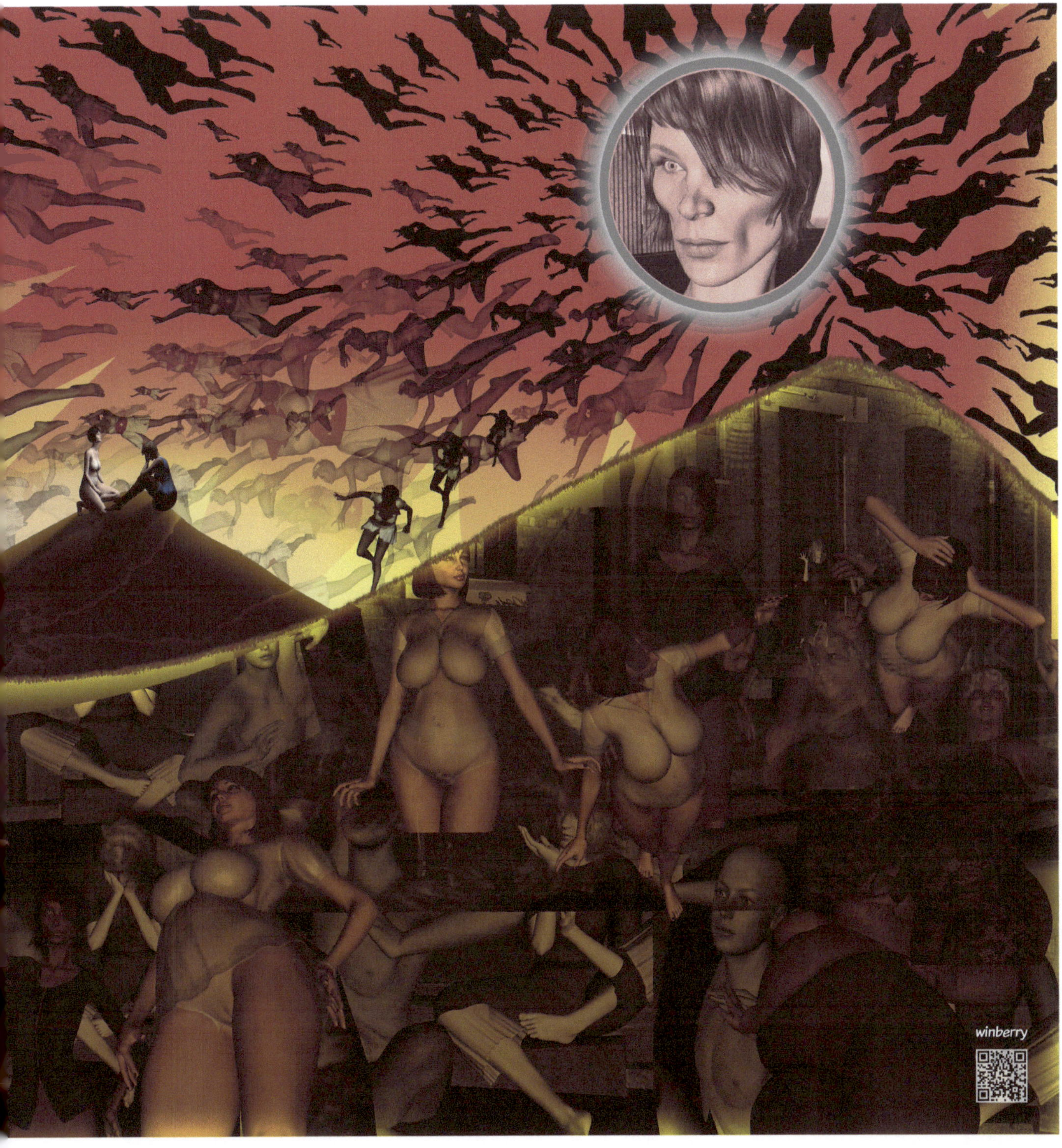
winberry

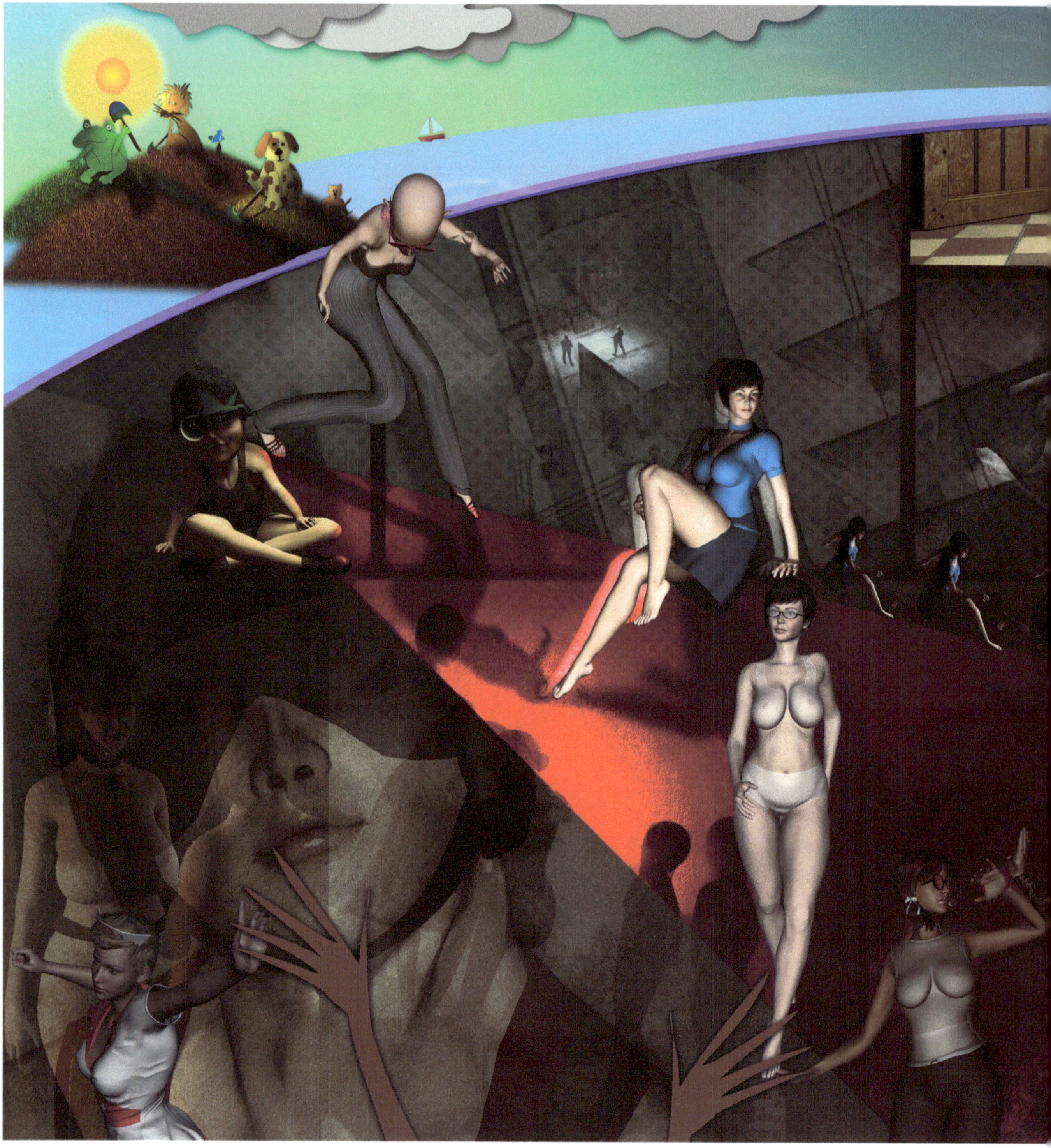

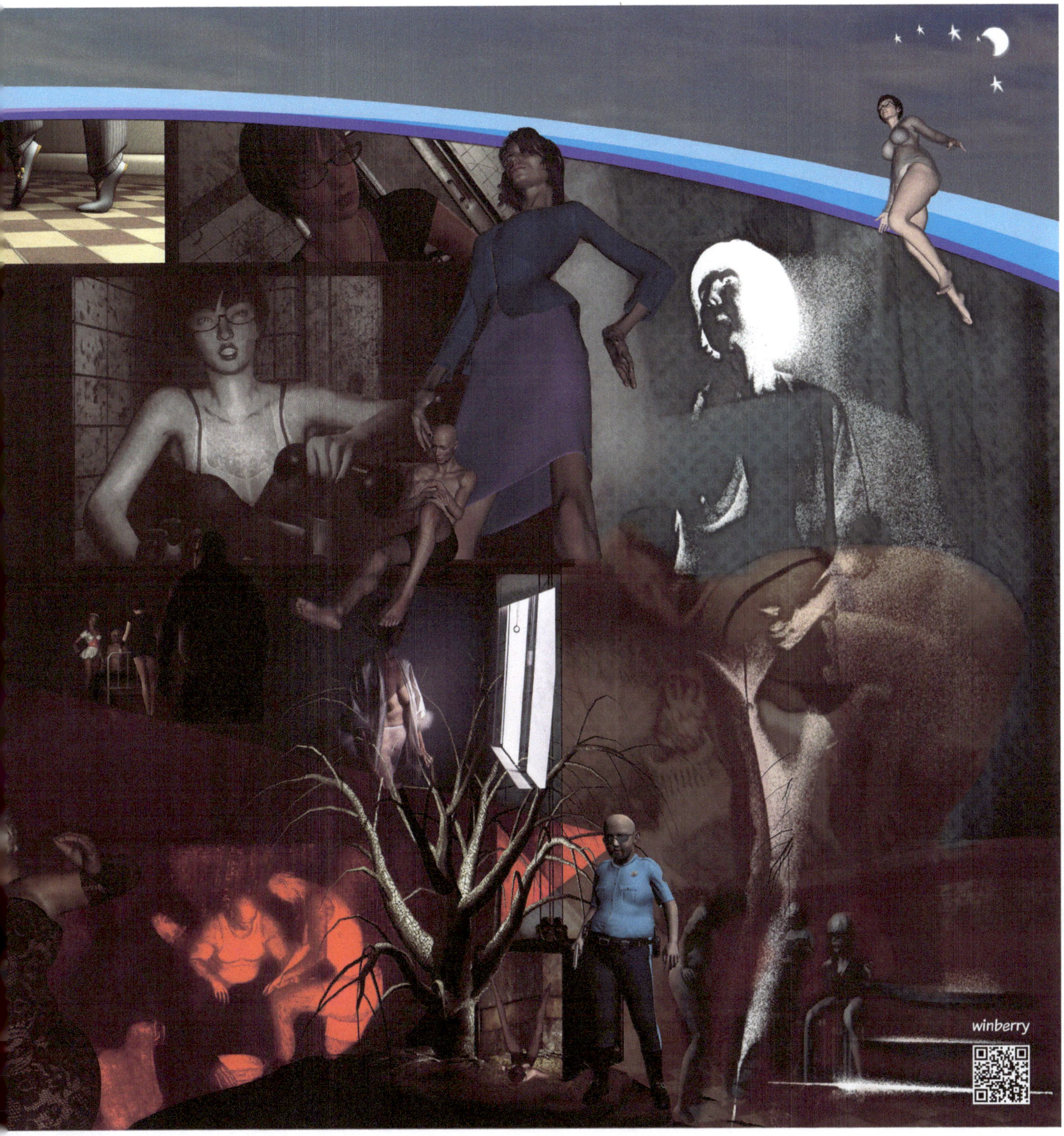
winberry

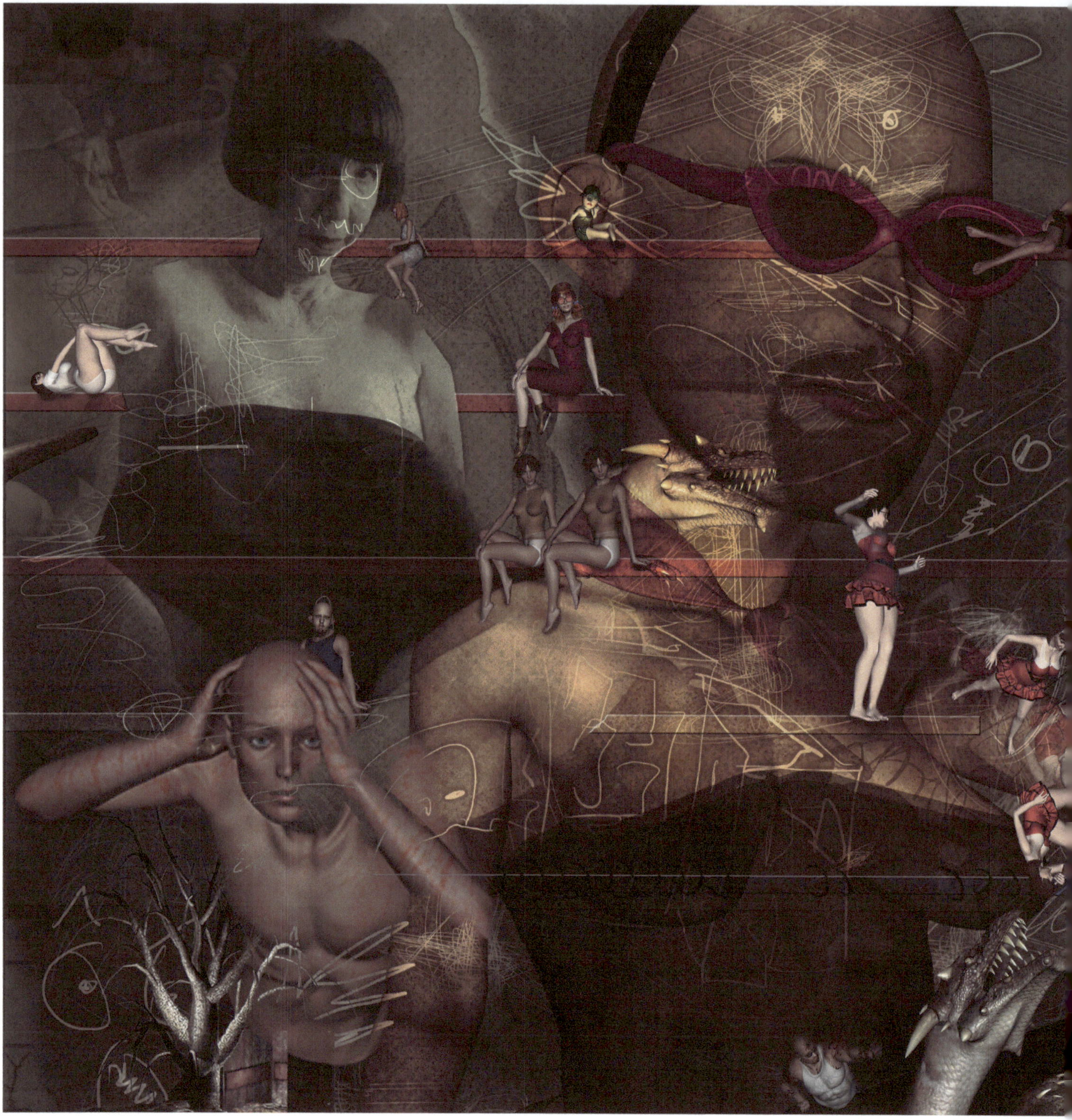

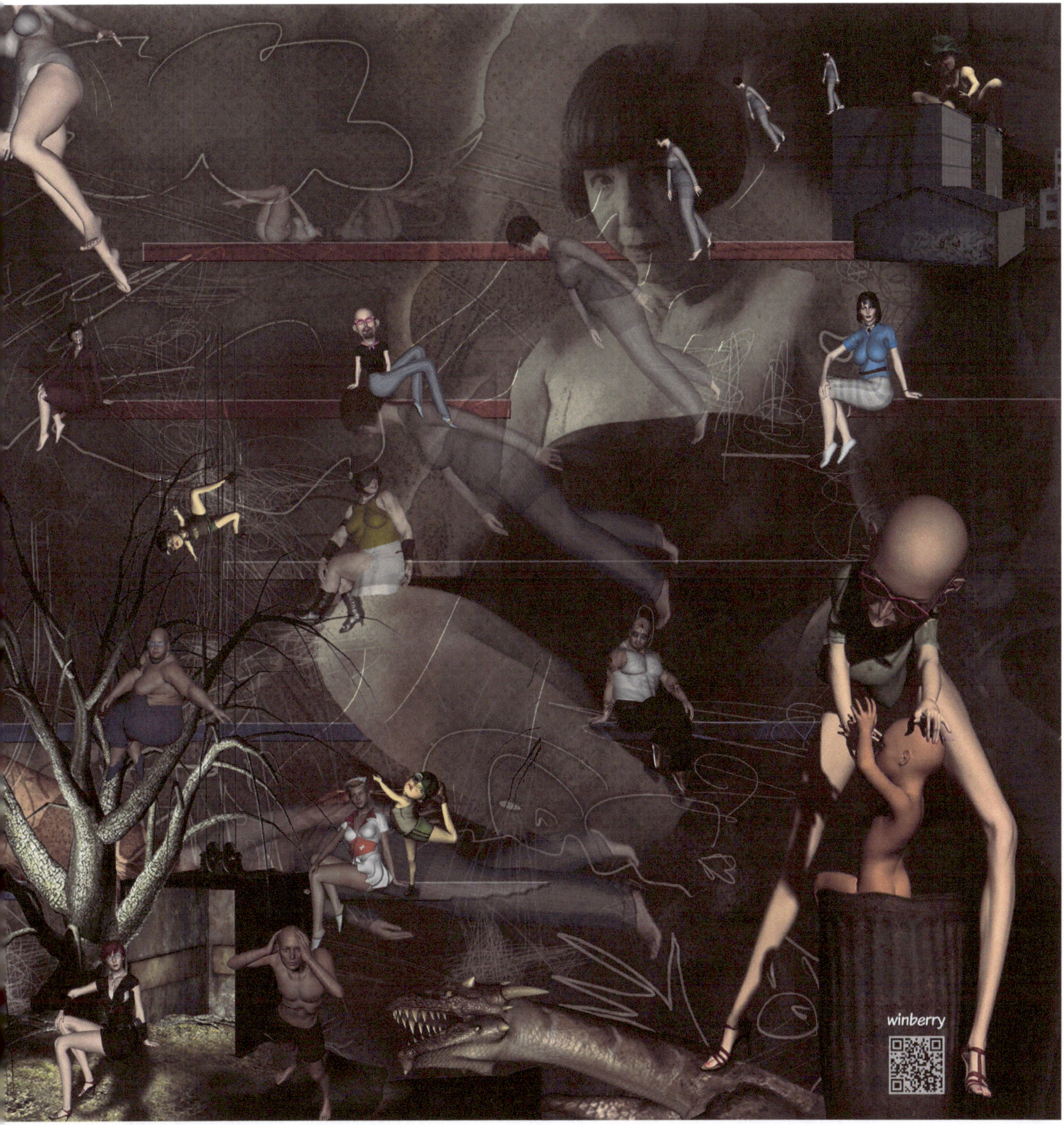
winberry

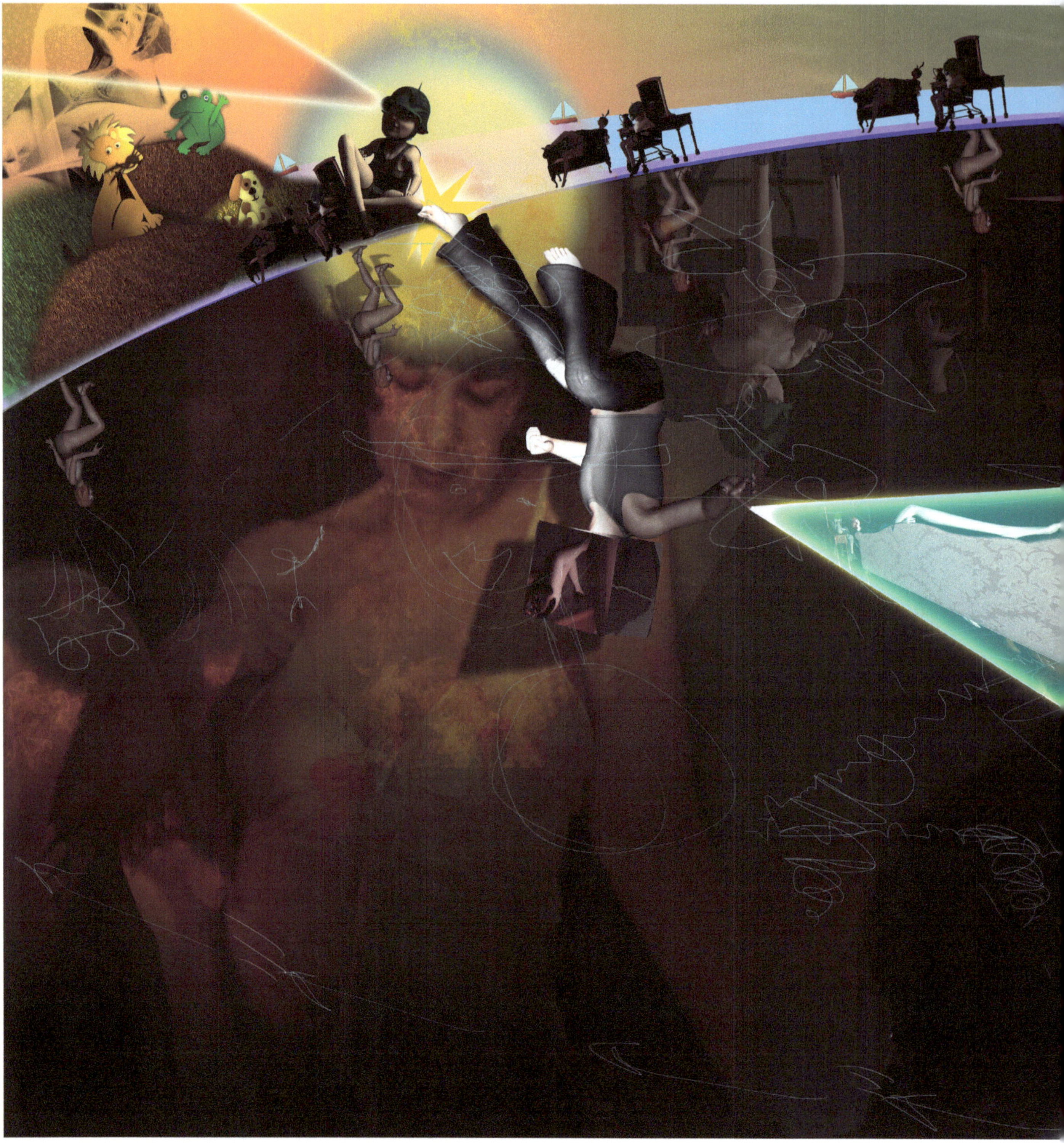

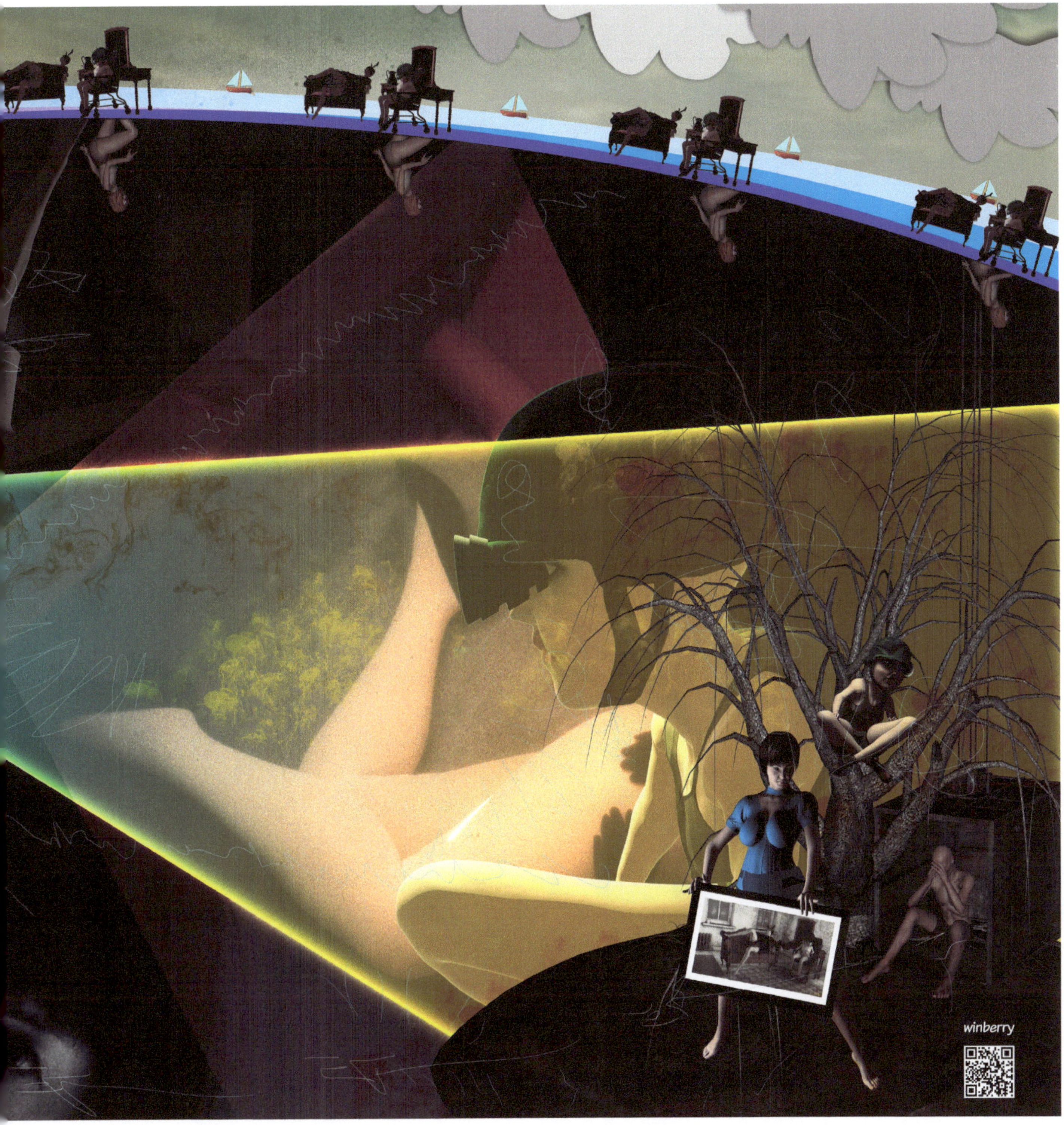
winberry

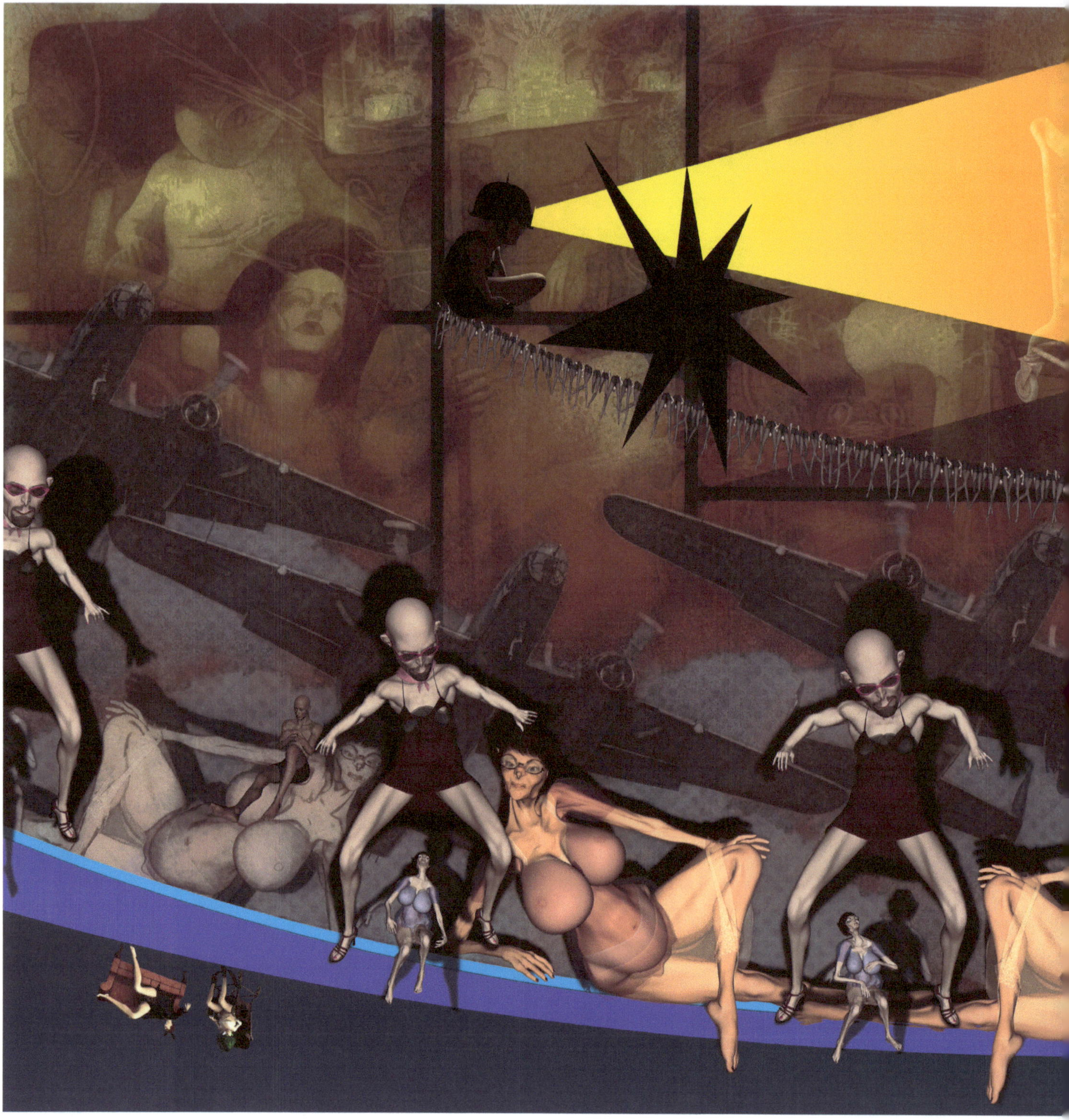

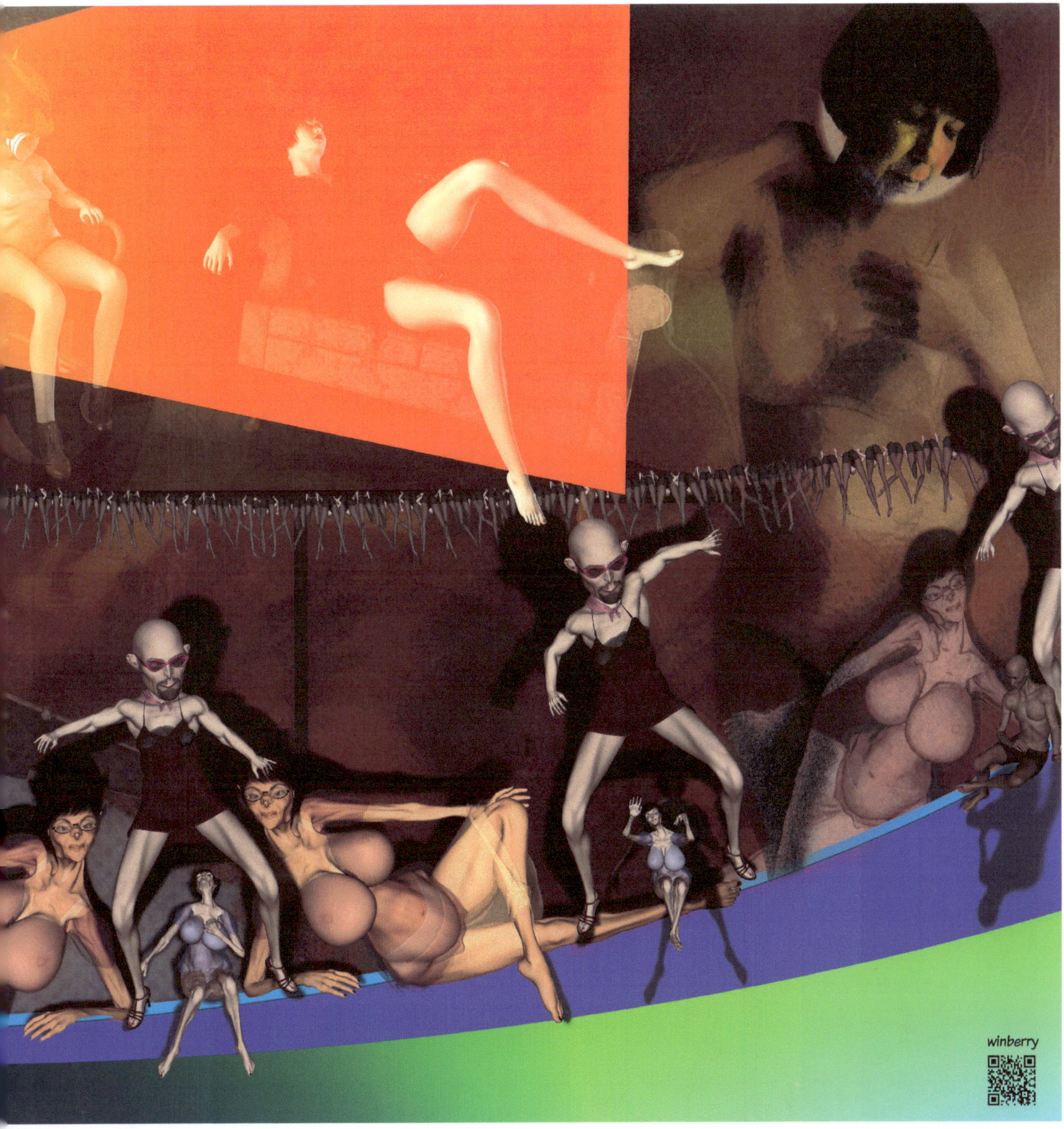
winberry

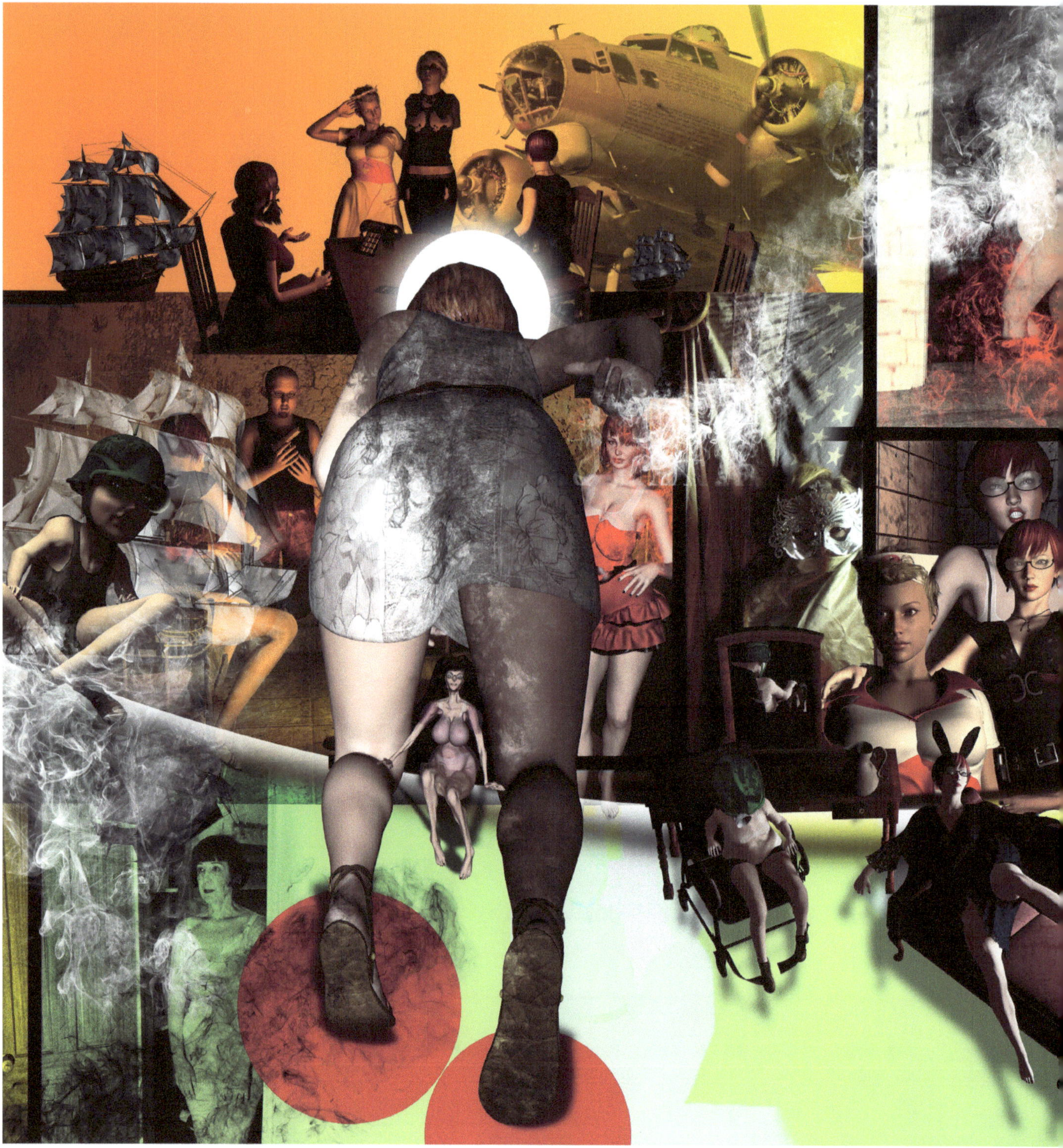

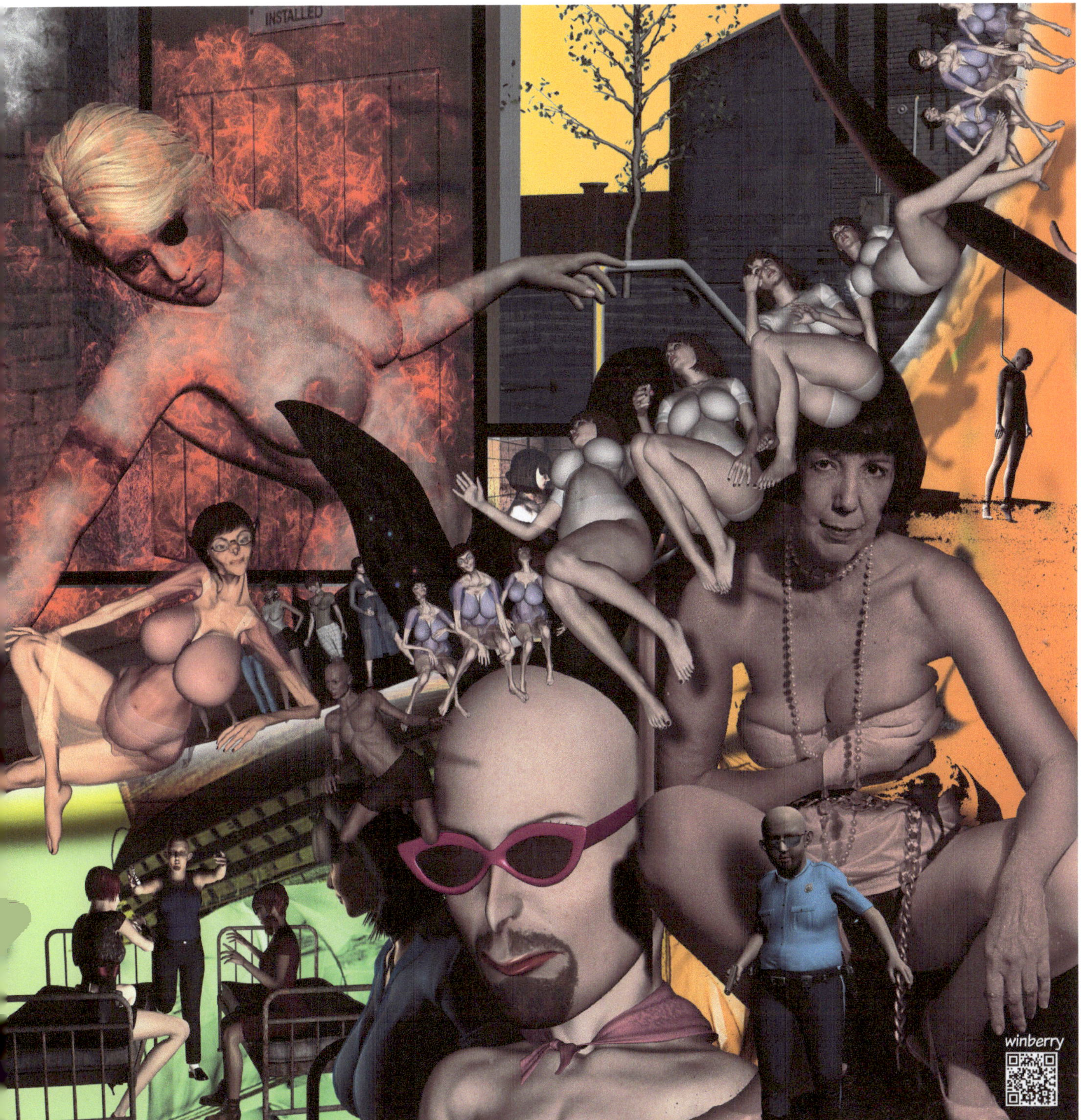
INSTALLED
winberry

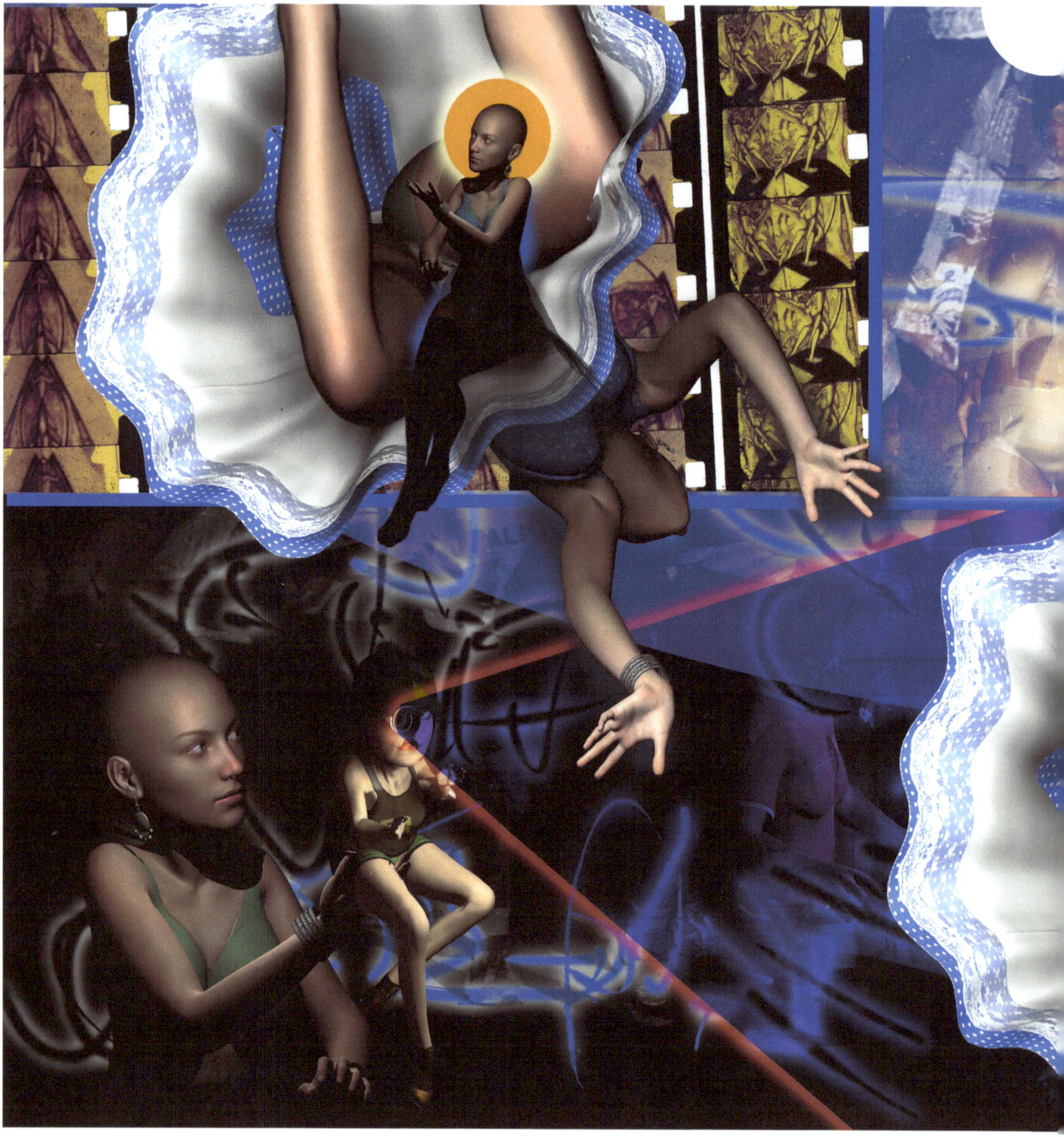

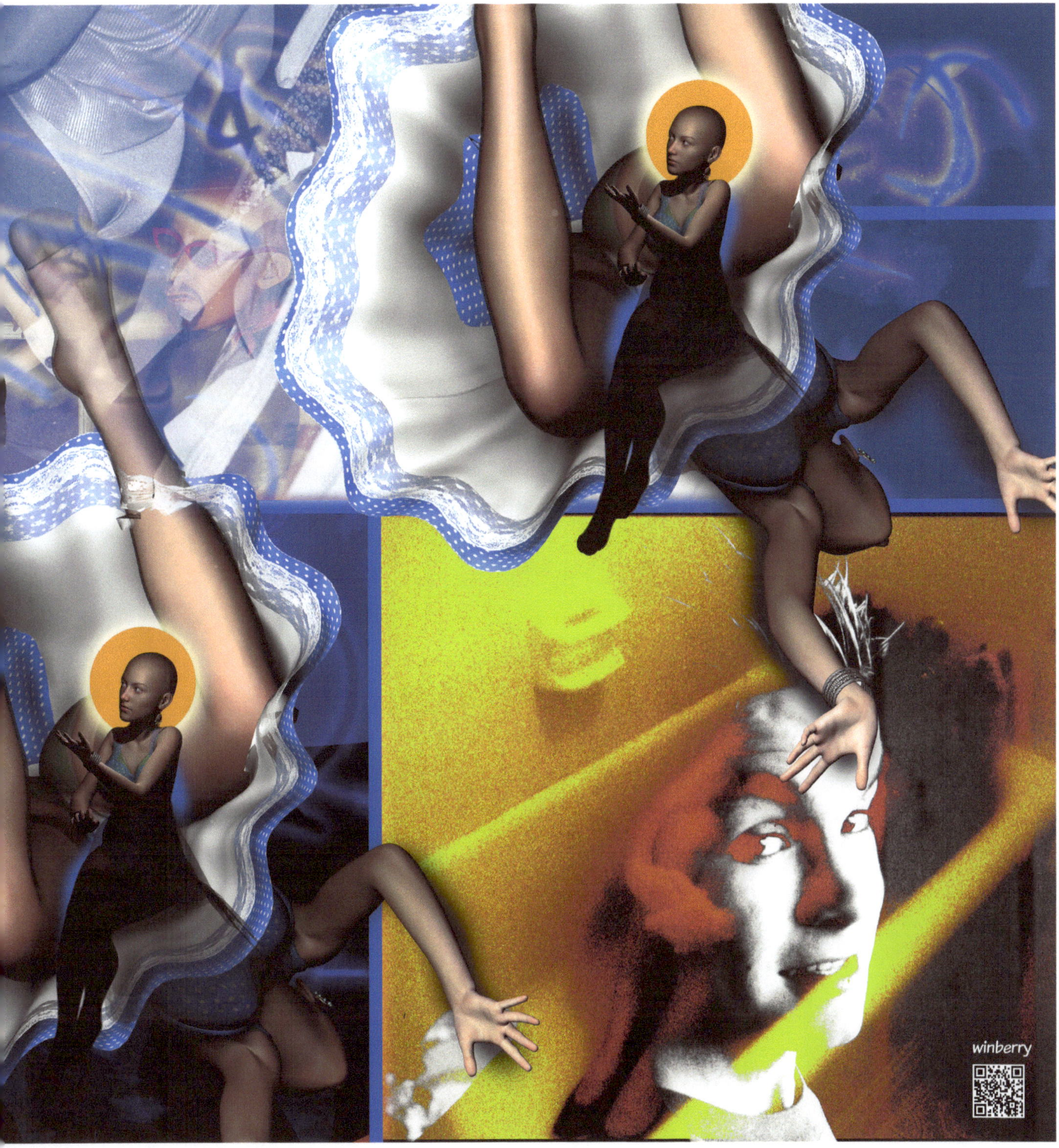
winberry

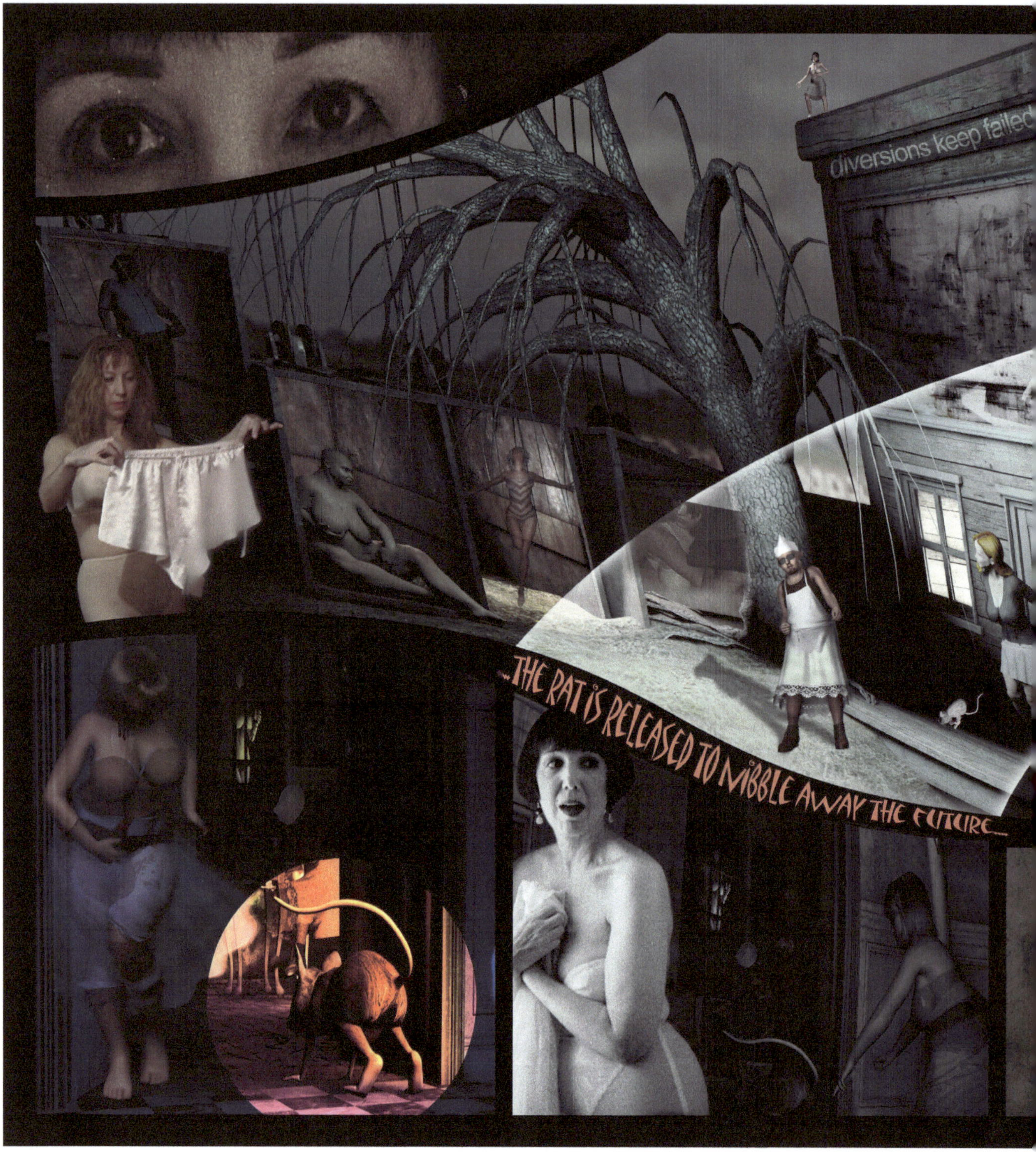
diversions keep failed
...THE RAT IS RELEASED TO NIBBLE AWAY THE FUTURE...

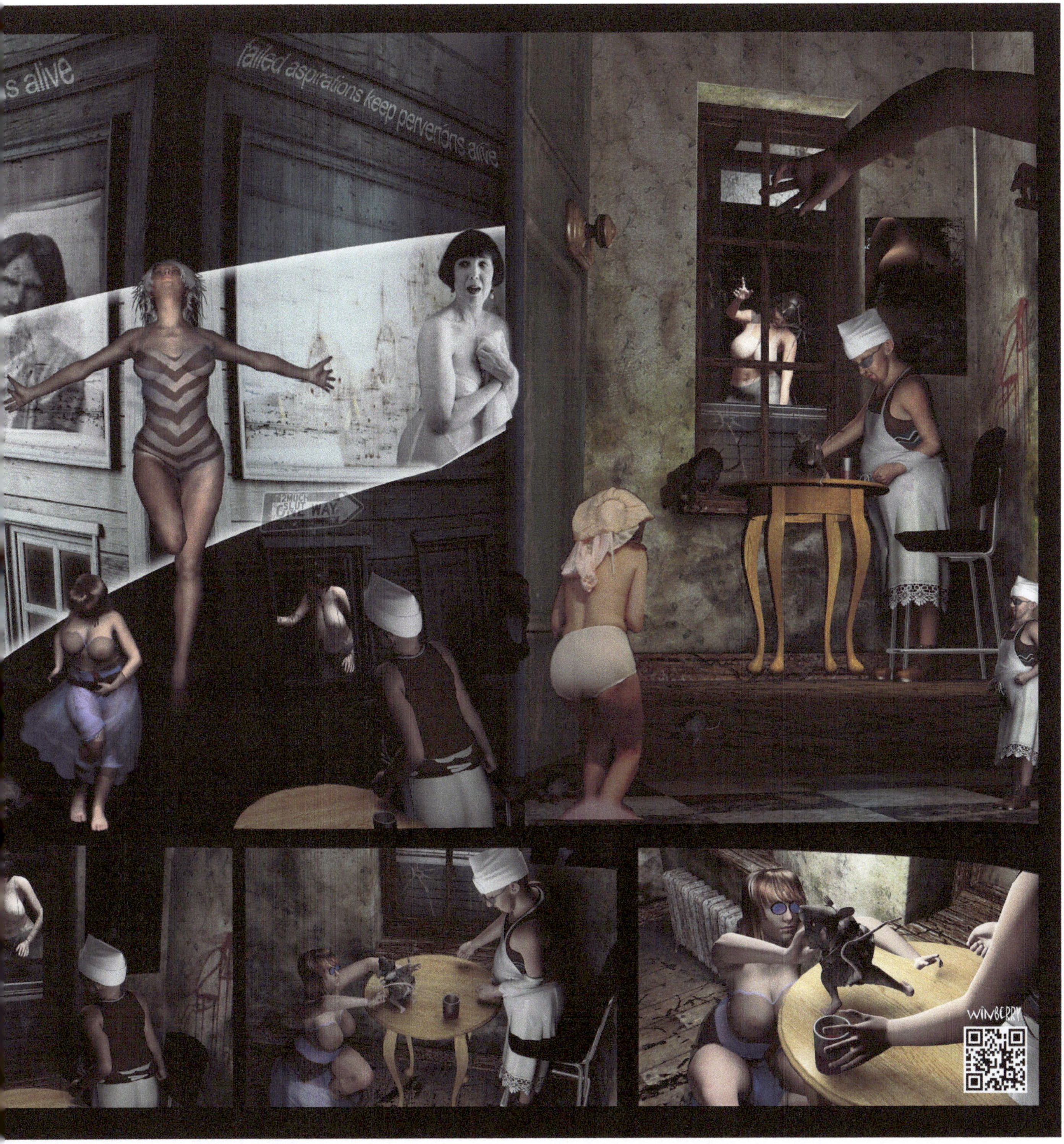
s alive
failed aspirations keep perverions alive
2MUCH
SLUT
ONE WAY
WINBERRY

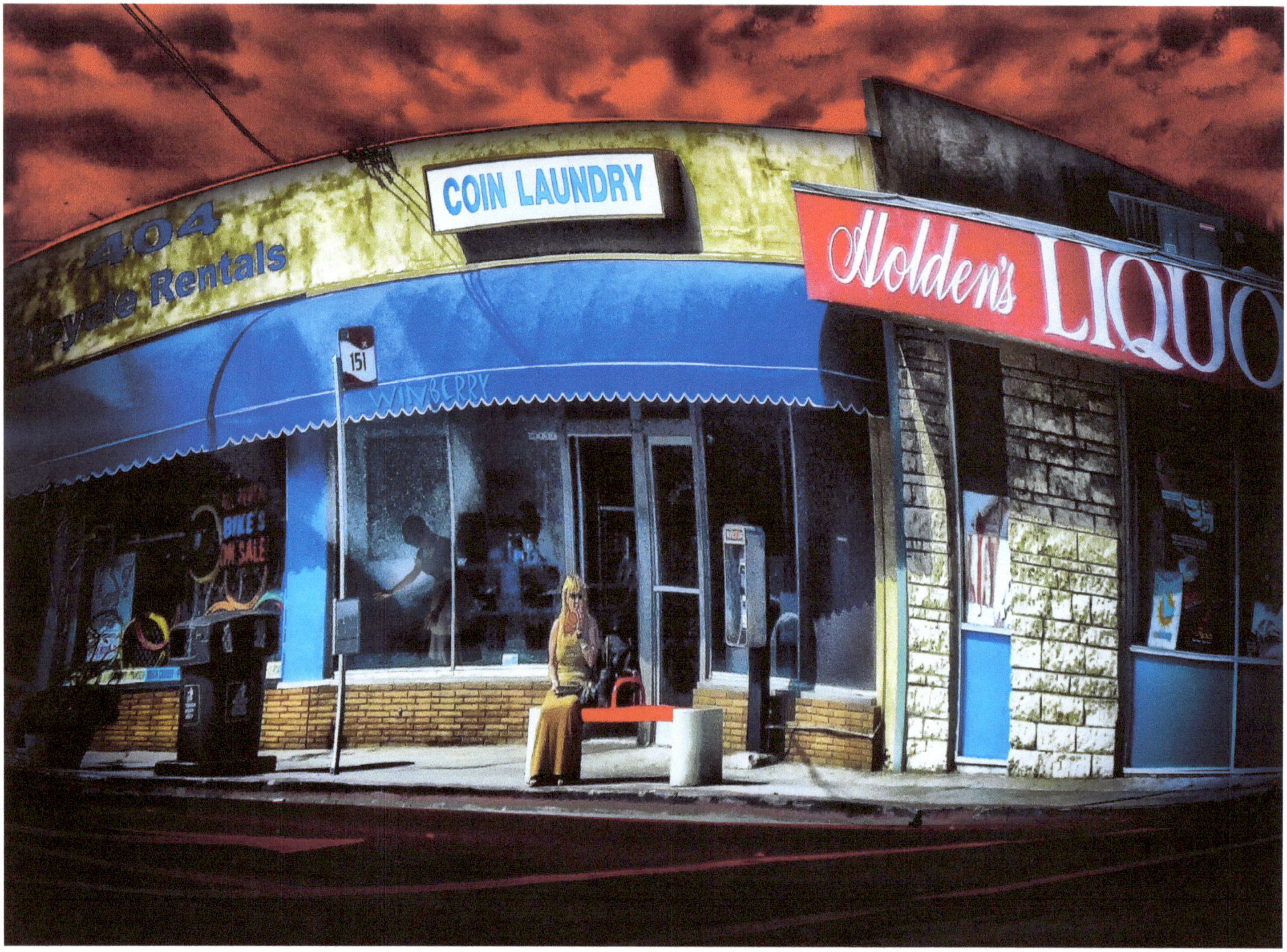
COIN LAUNDRY
404
Bicycle Rentals
Holden's LIQUO
151
WINBERRY

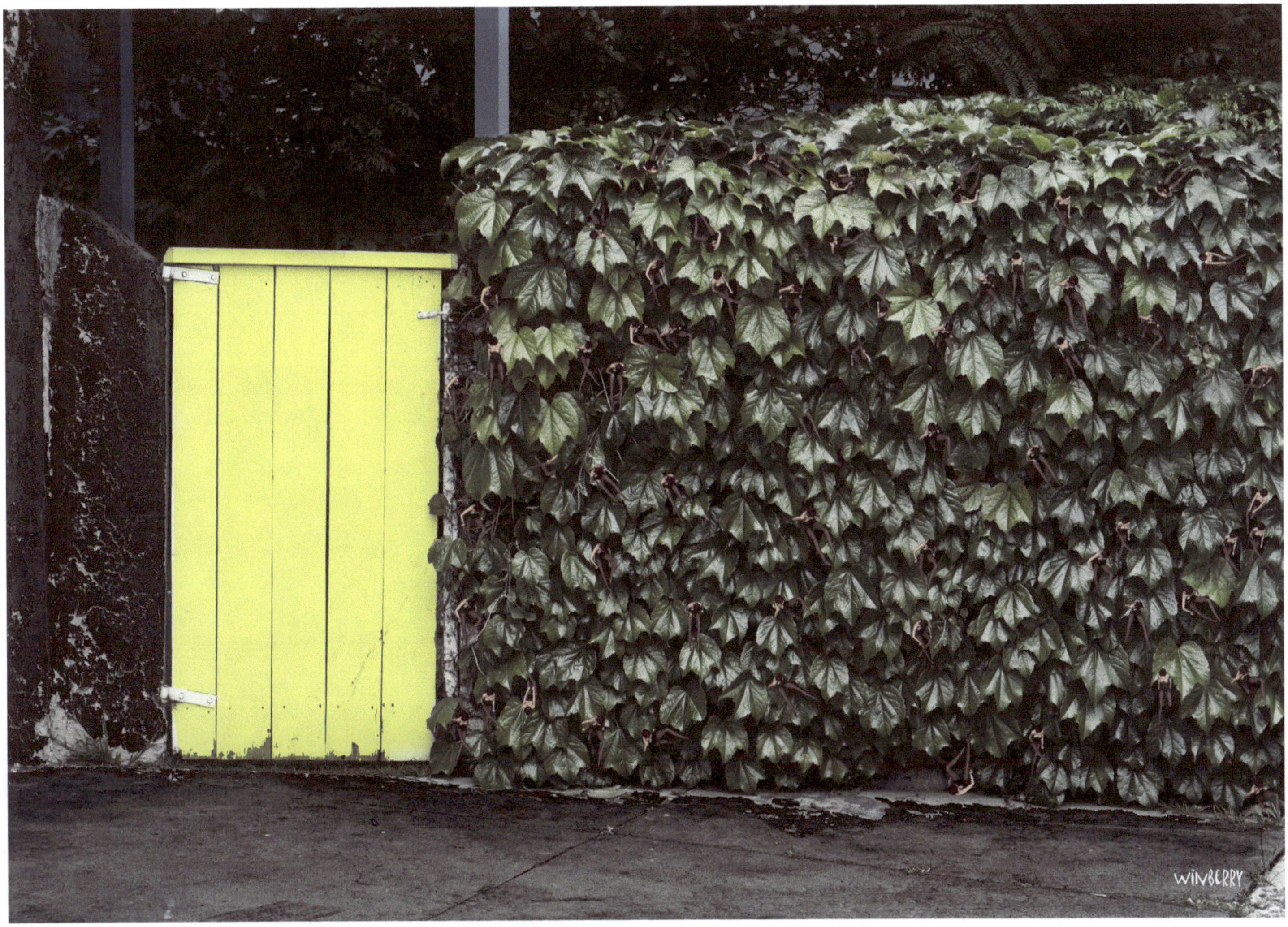
WINBERRY

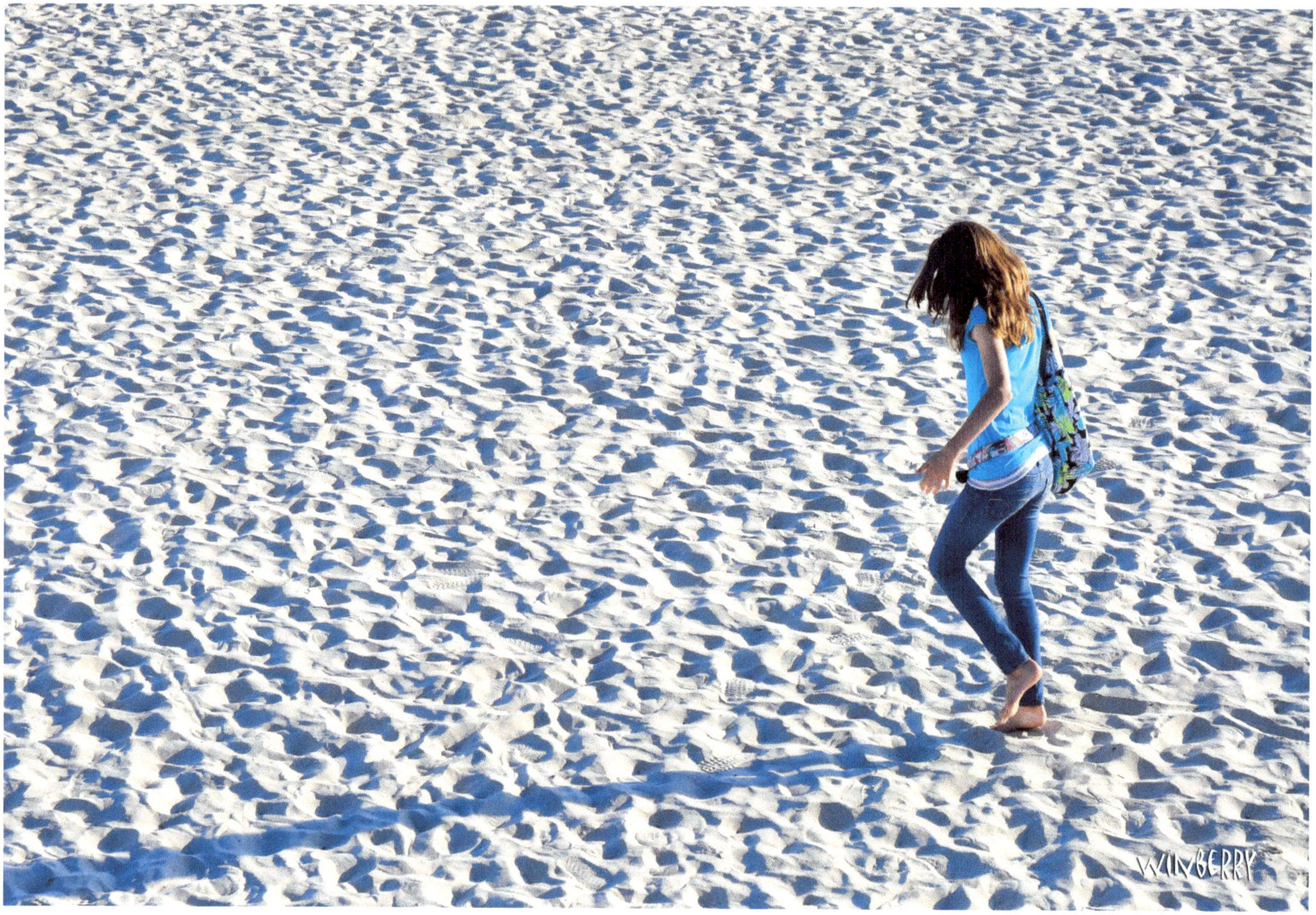
WINBERRY

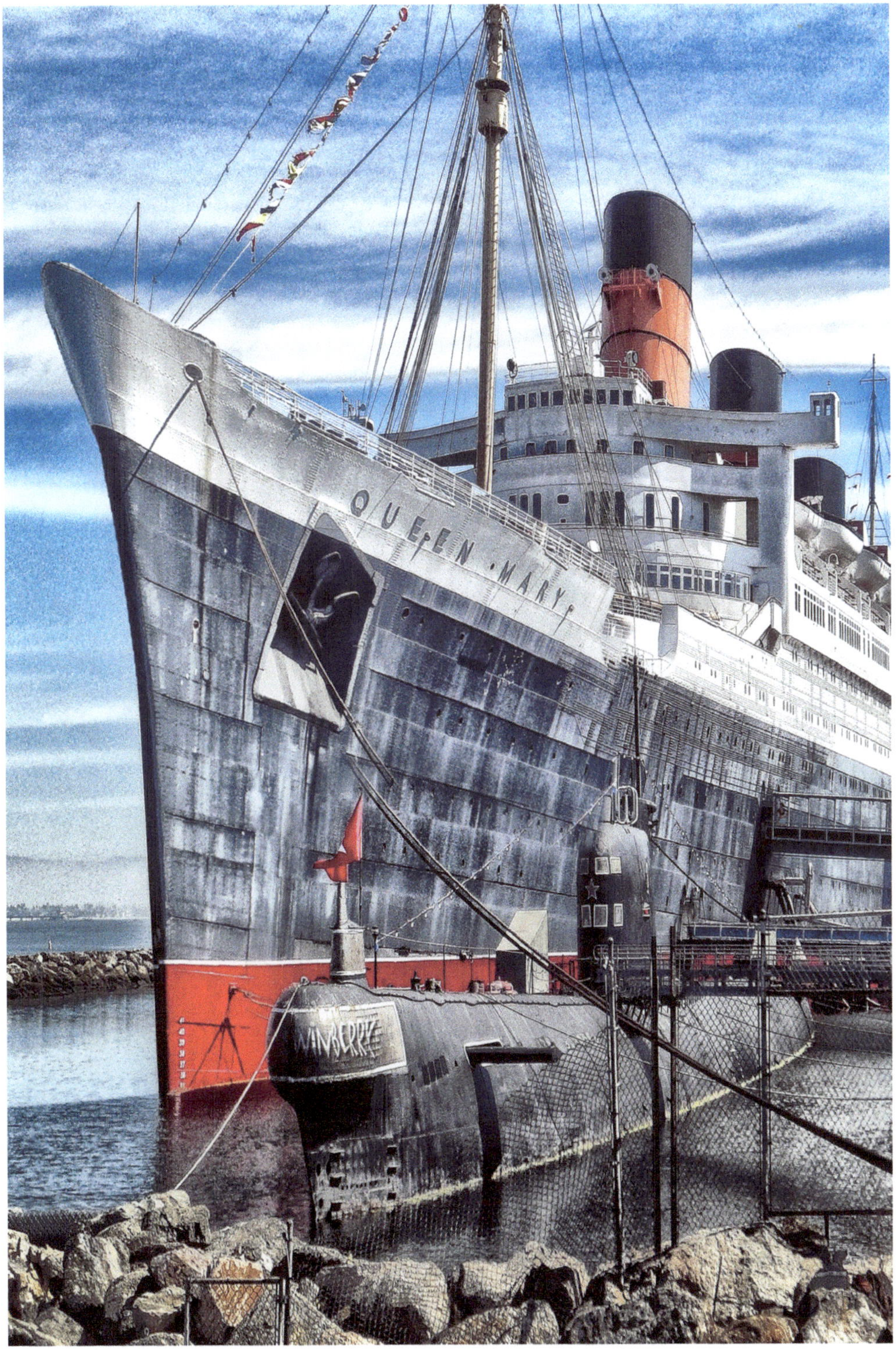
QUEEN MARY

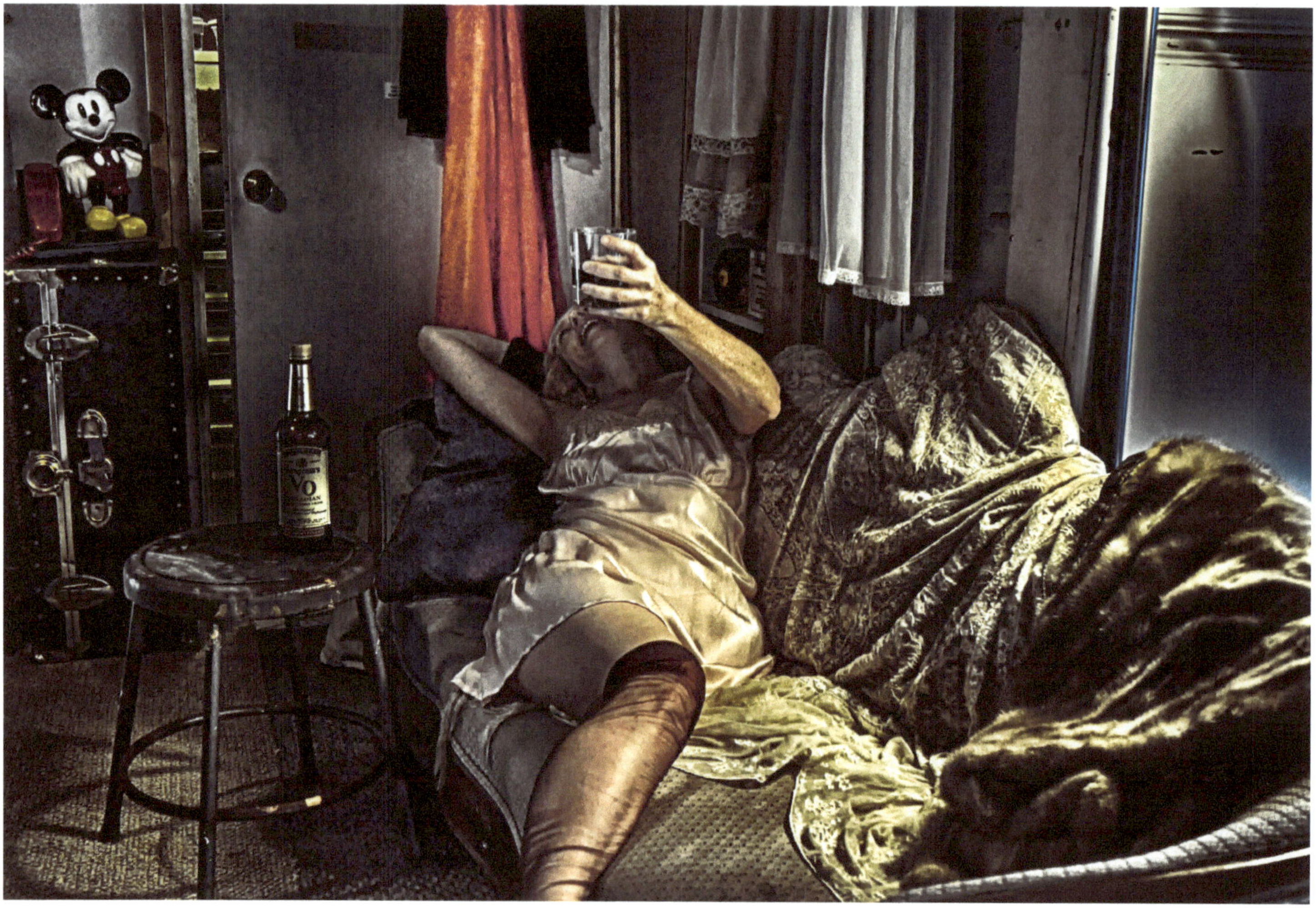
VO

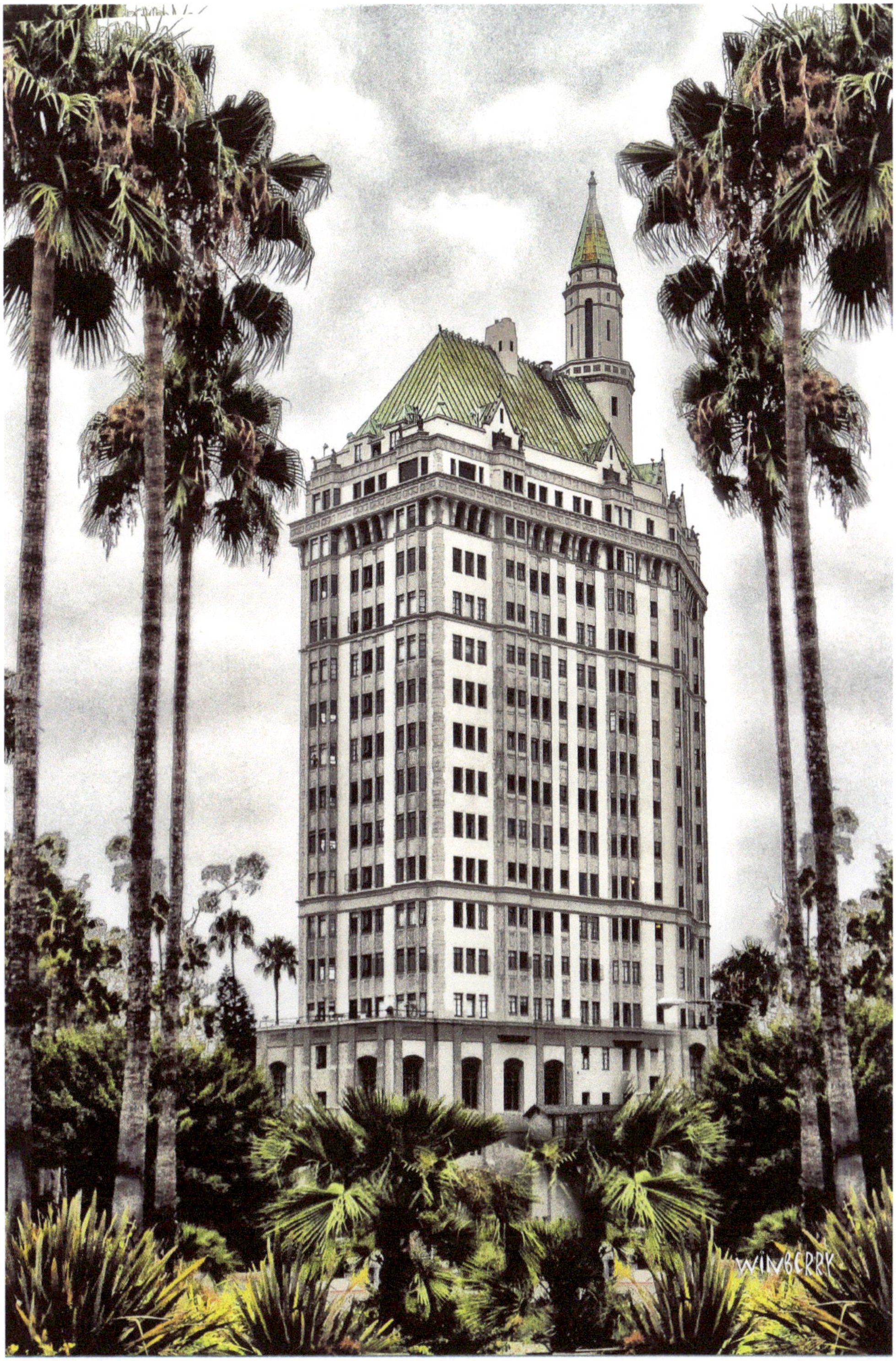
WINBERRY

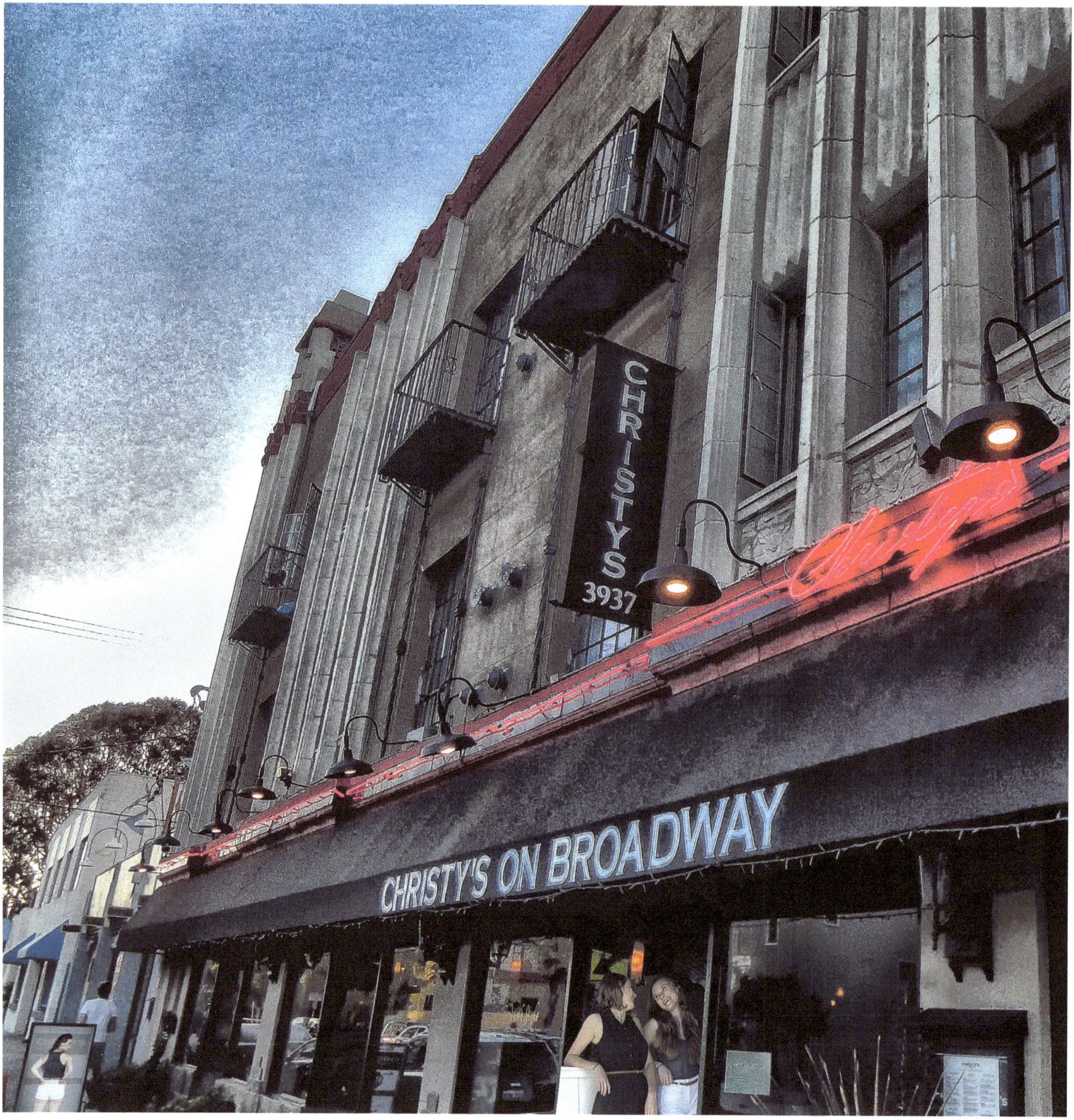
CHRISTYS
3937
CHRISTY'S ON BROADWAY

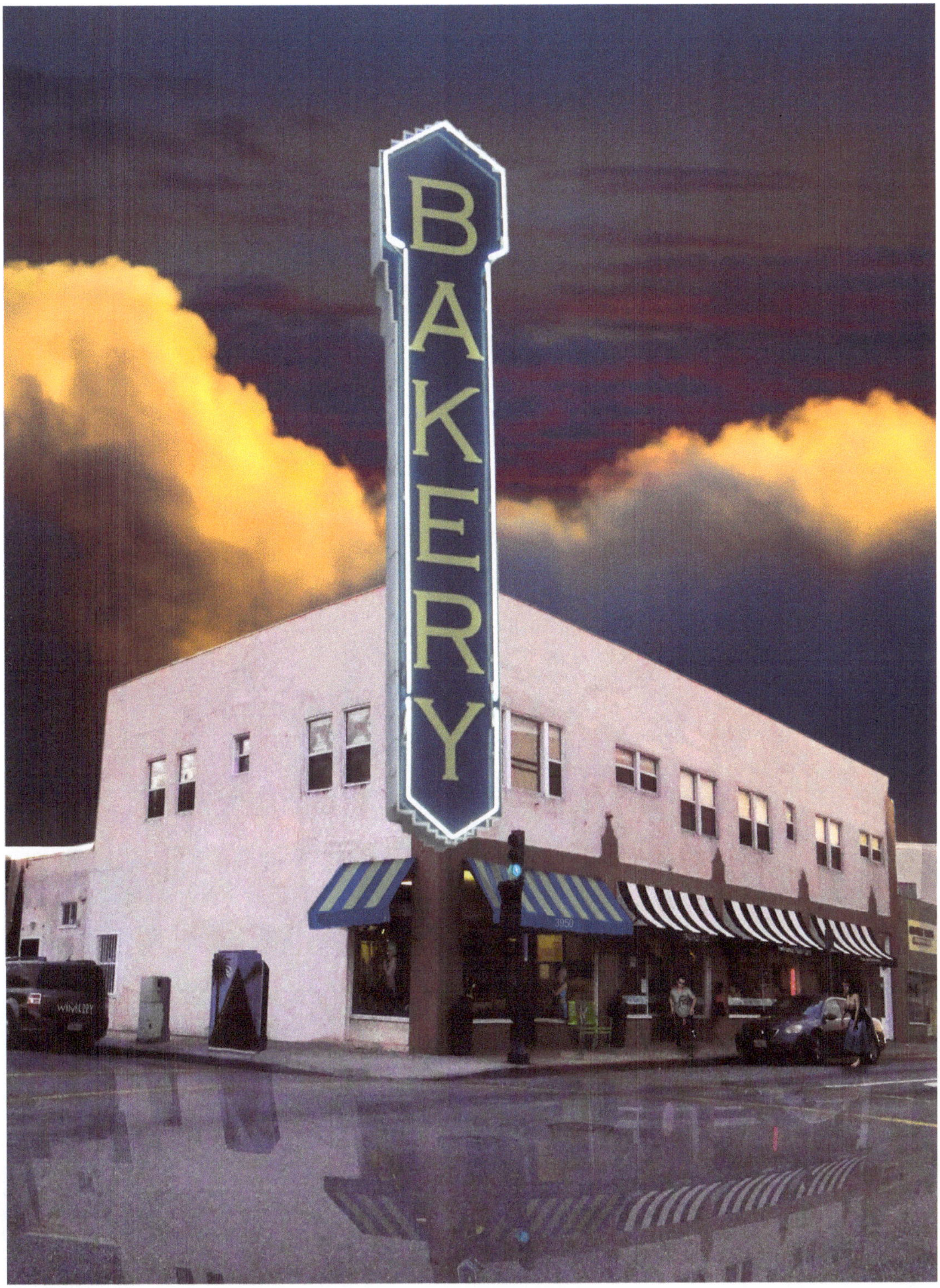
BAKERY

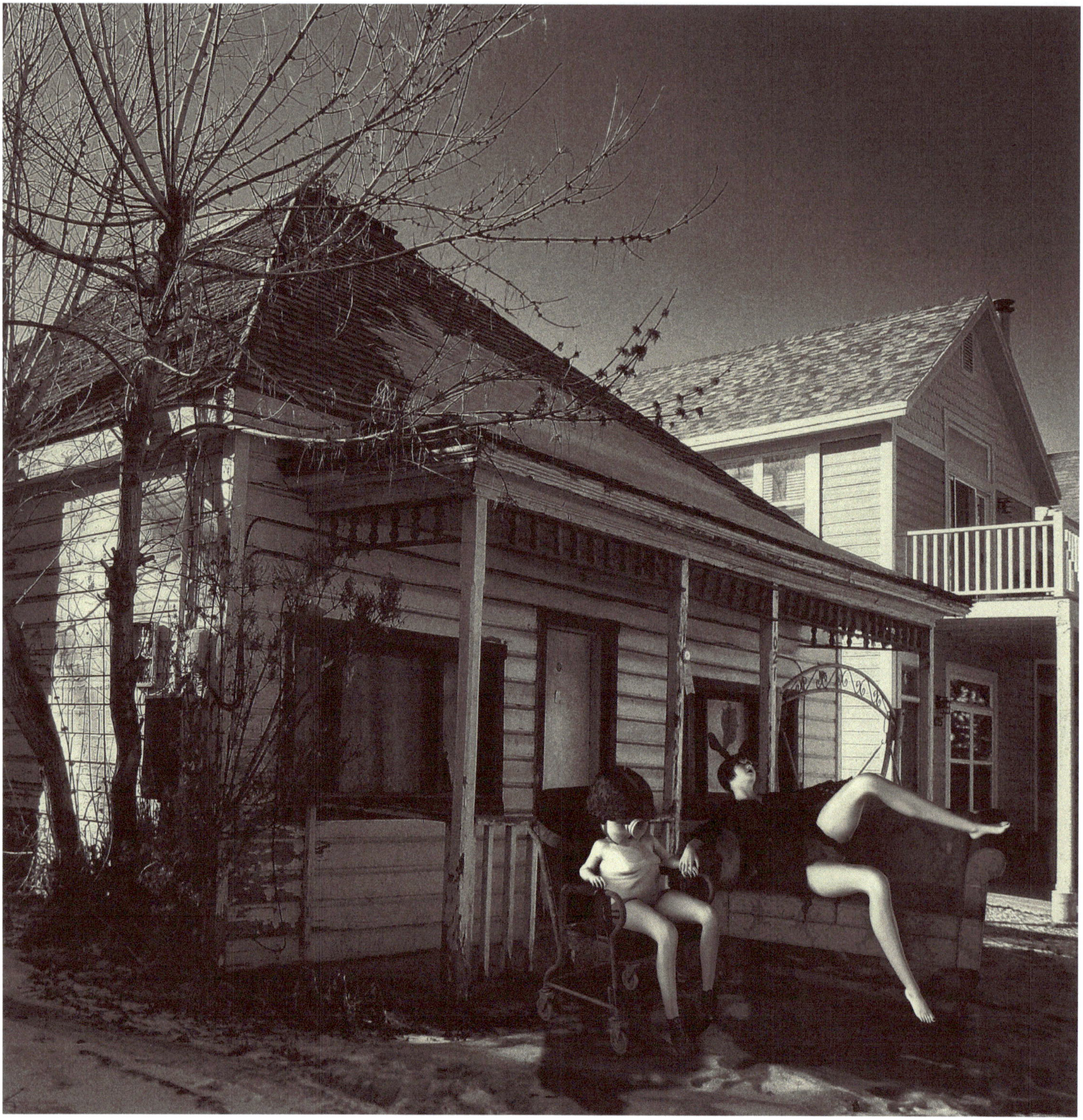

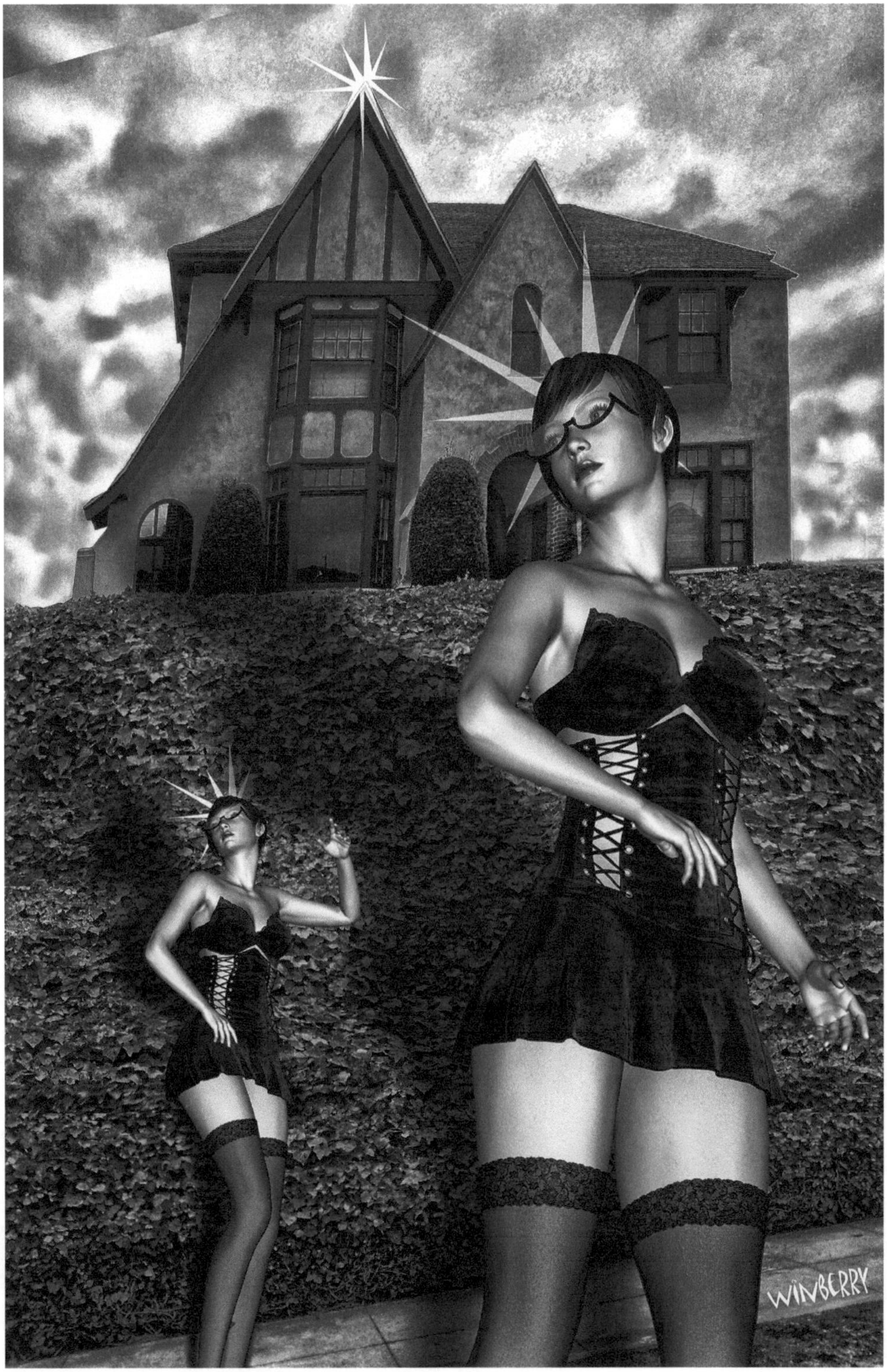
WINBERRY

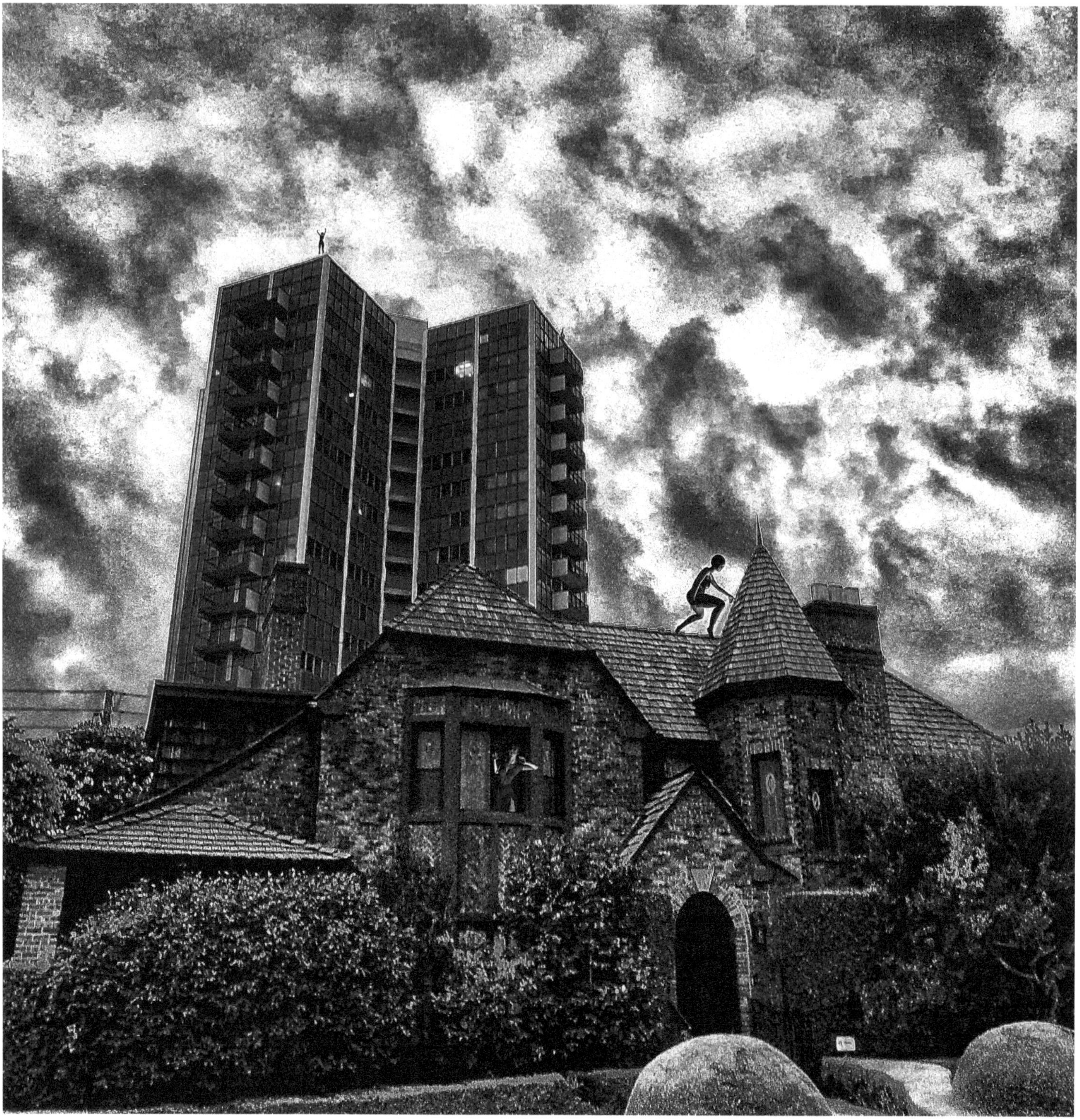

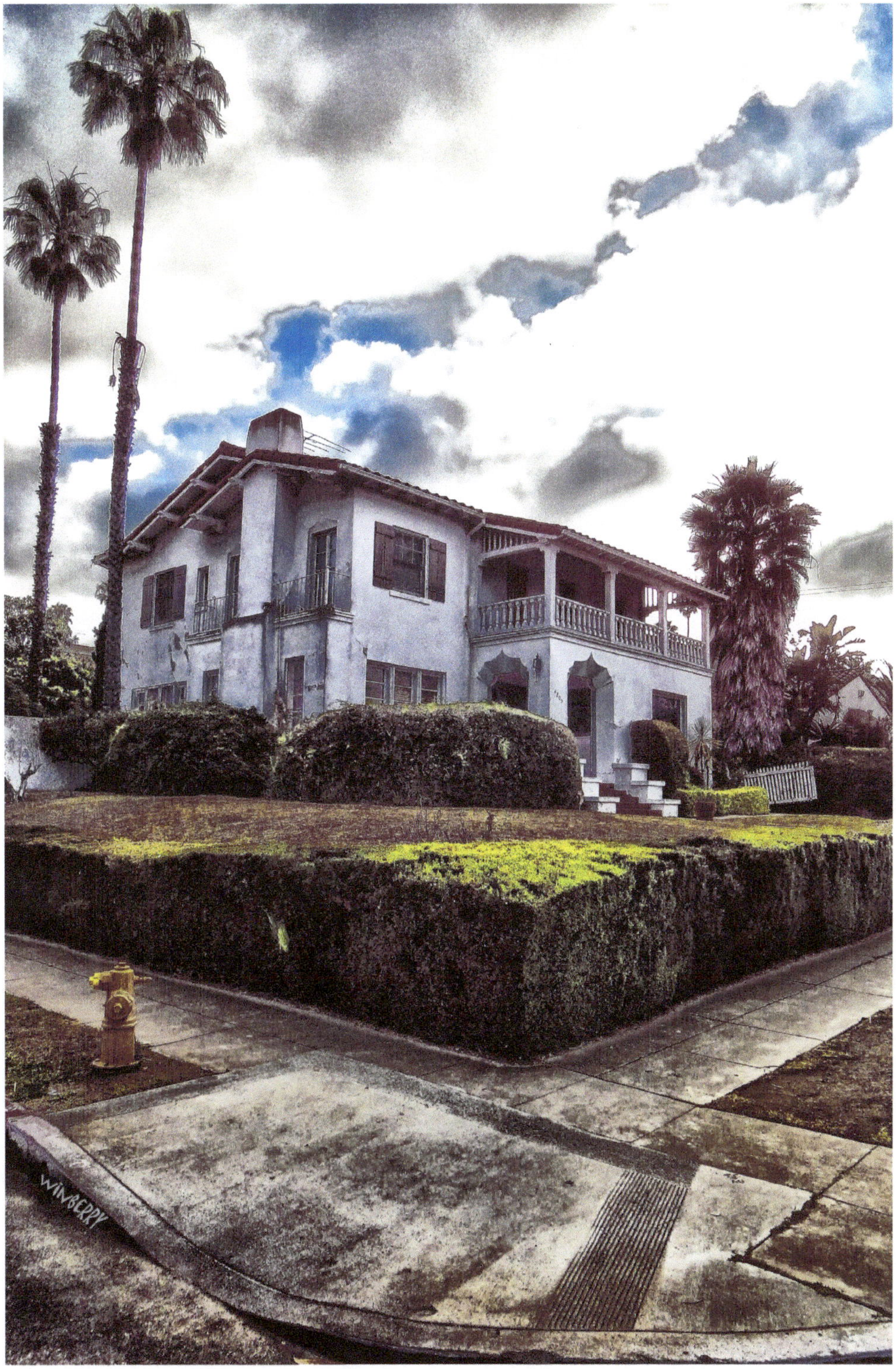
WINBERRY

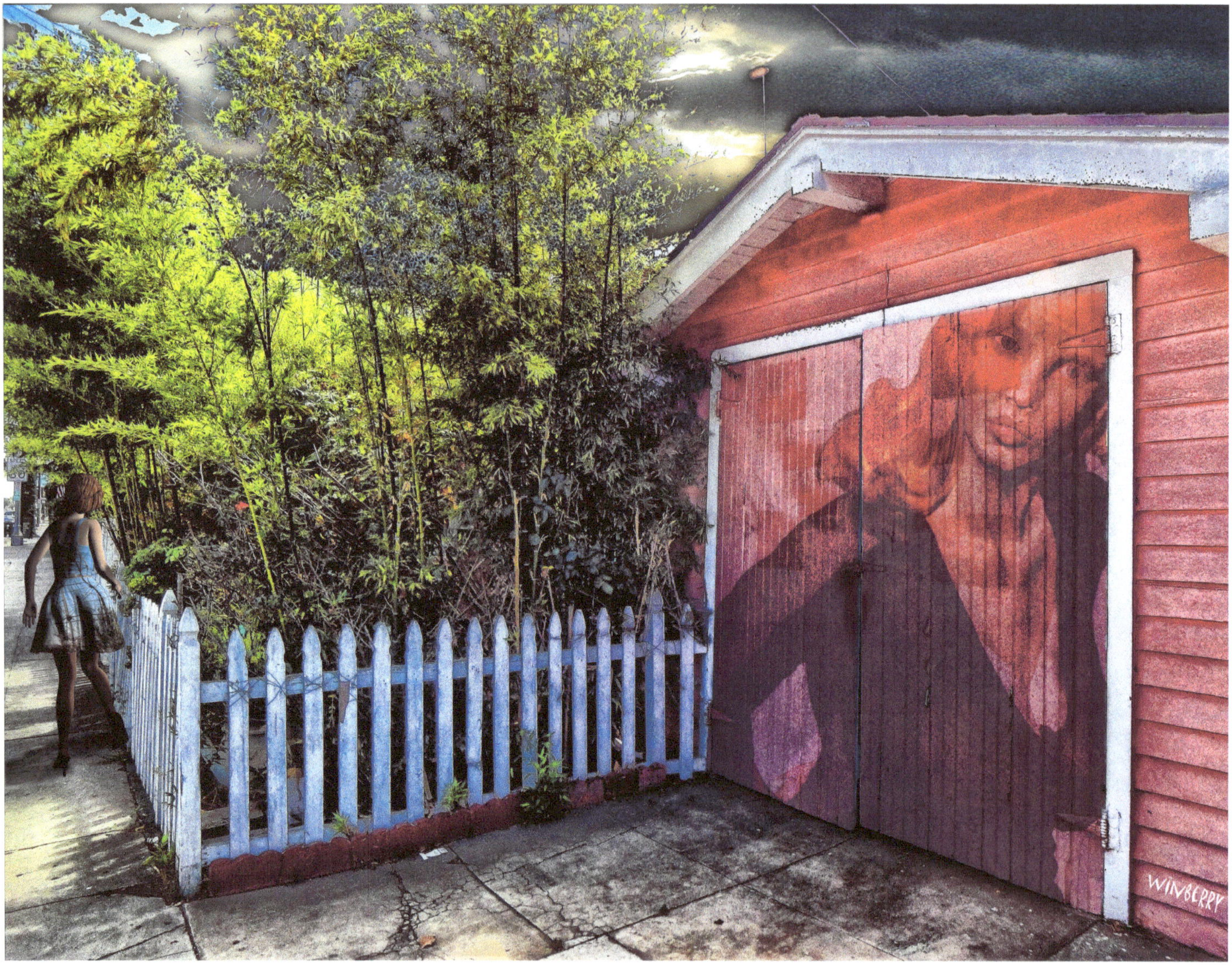
WINBERRY

www.ingramcontent.com/pod-product-compliance
Lightning Source LLC
Chambersburg PA
CBHW050758180526
45159CB00003B/1499
9781495305092